D1714698

CARNIVORES

MEAT~EATING MAMMALS

THE BRITANNICA GUIDE TO PREDATORS AND PREY

CARNIVORES
MEAT-EATING MAMMALS

EDITED BY JOHN P. RAFFERTY, ASSOCIATE EDITOR, EARTH AND LIFE SCIENCES

Educational Publishing

IN ASSOCIATION WITH

EDUCATIONAL SERVICES

Published in 2011 by Britannica Educational Publishing
(a trademark of Encyclopædia Britannica, Inc.)
in association with Rosen Educational Services, LLC
29 East 21st Street, New York, NY 10010.

First Edition

Britannica Educational Publishing
Michael I. Levy: Executive Editor
J.E. Luebering: Senior Manager
Marilyn L. Barton: Senior Coordinator, Production Control
Steven Bosco: Director, Editorial Technologies
Lisa S. Braucher: Senior Producer and Data Editor
Yvette Charboneau: Senior Copy Editor
Kathy Nakamura: Manager, Media Acquisition
John P. Rafferty: Associate Editor, Earth and Life Sciences

Rosen Educational Services
Hope Lourie Killcoyne: Senior Editor and Project Manager
Nelson Sá: Art Director
Cindy Reiman: Photography Manager
Matthew Cauli: Designer, Cover Design
Introduction by Cathy Vanderhoof

Library of Congress Cataloging-in-Publication Data

Carnivores : meat-eating mammals / edited by John P. Rafferty.
    p. cm. — (The Britannica guide to predators and prey)
"In association with Britannica Educational Publishing, Rosen Educational Services."
Includes bibliographical references and index.
ISBN 978-1-61530-340-3 (library binding)
    1. Carnivora—Juvenile literature. I. Rafferty, John P.
QL737.C2C347 2011
599.7—dc22

                                                                    2010033864

Manufactured in the United States of America

On the cover: A mature male lion (*Panthera leo*). *Steve Allen/Photodisc/Getty Images*

On page x: The least weasel is the smallest living carnivore. *Shutterstock.com*

On pp. v–ix and xviii: Alaskan brown bear. *Roy Toft/National Geographic Image Collection/Getty Images*

Pages 1, 15, 45, 78, 130, 154, 185 Siberian tiger. iStockphoto/Thinkstock; pages 1, 15, 45, 78, 130,
154, 185, 244, 277, 282, 287 Banner. © www.istockphoto.com/Vladimir Sazonov

CONTENTS

1

17

49

65

79

96

123

136

147

156

174

191

215

223

234

"Lions and tigers and bears, oh my!" chants Dorothy as she enters the forest of Oz in the classic film *The Wizard of Oz* (1939). Although you would never actually find all three of these creatures in the same habitat, they are indeed among the small number of carnivorous animals that will attack humans. Carnivores, whose diets are primarily made up of the flesh of other animals, are part of the order Carnivora. However, not all carnivores are threats to humans. In addition to lions, tigers, and bears, the order also includes domestic cats and dogs, as well as otters, foxes, raccoons, meerkats, and a variety of other species. Members of order Carnivora occupy important niches in the ecosystems they inhabit, and some species even serve as top predators.

Many types of birds, reptiles, and fish are also flesh-eating predators, and even some plants are flesh-eaters. However, from a taxonomic perspective, all members of order Carnivora are mammals. Although some aquatic mammals, such as the seals and walruses, are also typically included in order Carnivora, this book presents a detailed study of the terrestrial families of carnivores. Terrestrial carnivores include the Canidae (dogs and related species), Felidae (cats), Ursidae (bears), Procyonidae (raccoons and related species), Mustelidae (weasels, badgers, otters, and related species), Mephitidae (skunks and stink badgers), Herpestidae (mongooses), Viverridae (civets, genets, and related species), and Hyaenidae (hyenas).

Carnivores play an important role in the environment by limiting the populations of the species they prey upon, thus maintaining the balance between the available resources and the populations dependent on those resources within a given ecosystem. Human encroachment on their territories has resulted in a variety of outcomes. In some cases, humans have eliminated or attempted to eliminate animals that prey on domestic livestock or important game animals. Without the checks provided by top carnivores, the populations of prey species, such as white-tailed deer in North America, rise quickly. Prey populations in ecosystems devoid of large carnivores are only limited by their food supply. In such ecosystems, plants are browsed more heavily. In addition, populations of smaller carnivores, such as racoons, coyotes, and foxes, also increase dramatically, because top carnivores are no longer present to interfere with their activities. In other cases, human settlement has disrupted the carnivores' natural territories, sometimes to the extent that the carnivore population is eliminated from the region. However, some species, such as the aforementioned smaller carnivores, and even some species of bears, actually adapt to life in suburban and urban areas. Over the course of time, certain carnivore species have been domesticated by humans. Dogs, cats, and even ferrets provide companionship to humans as household pets.

The largest terrestrial carnivores can be found among the bear family. (The Kodiak and polar bears of the Arctic region are the largest bears.) Bears range throughout North America, Europe, and Asia. The spectacled bear of the Andes Mountains is the only living bear found south of the equator. The only known African bear species, the Atlas bear, became extinct more than a century ago. Scientists believe that bears are the most recently evolved family of carnivores, splitting from the Canidae as recently as the Late Miocene Epoch (11.6 million to 5.3 million years ago).

Most bears fall under the genus Ursus, including Asiatic black bears, North American black bears, brown bears, grizzly bears, and polar bears. Other bears form their own unique genera, including the spectacled bear,

animals and were also valued for their useful function of protecting granaries from rodents.

Unlike many carnivorous species, which will eat plants, insects, and other available foods as well as meat, members of the cat family are almost entirely carnivorous. Most cats are solitary hunters, quietly stalking their prey and then attacking with a leap or quick, short run. Although cheetahs are credited as being the fastest mammals on Earth, cats are better suited to short sprints than the sustained long-distance running. (The canids are the endurance athletes of order Carnivora.) All cats can climb trees, and some species, such as the leopards, jaguars, and ocelots, spend much of their time there. Asia is home to some of the more unusual felines: the flat-headed cat is an extremely rare species that prefers fruit and sweet potatoes to supplement its diet of fish and frogs, whereas the fishing cat hunts by scooping its prey out of the water. Cats are generally nocturnal, with acute hearing and large eyes specially adapted for night vision, but their sense of smell is not as developed as that of the canids.

Smaller carnivore groups include the weasels and related species of the family Mustelidae. The mustelids make up 54 distinct species of ferrets, polecats, badgers, martens, otters, wolverines, and others. Of these, the largest terrestrial species is the wolverine, which can reach a size of about 1.2 metres (4 feet) in length and 23 kg (50 pounds) in weight, and sea otters, which are aquatic mustelids, can be even larger. Most members of the family, however, are far smaller. The smallest mustelid is the least weasel, which weighs less than an ounce.

The common ferret is the most domesticated species in this group. Used for hunting since at least Roman times, they serve as popular pets today. The closely related black-footed ferret was thought to be extinct until the discovery of a small population in Wyoming in 1981. It is still considered highly endangered, even though a program of captive breeding and reintroduction has re-established populations in the western United States and Mexico. Some members of the weasel family, such as mink and ermine, are also prized for their fur and are often raised in captivity for that purpose.

Other carnivores include hyenas, raccoons and their relatives (the coatis and kinkajous), skunks, stink badgers, meerkats, and mongooses. The viverrids, a group that includes civets and related species, are also placed in the ranks of small carnivores. Many have adapted extremely well to human presence. For example, the highest population densities of some species, such as raccoons, are actually in large cities where most of the diet is obtained from scavenging rather than hunting. Skunks are welcome predators in agricultural areas where they kill insects and rodents that can damage crops and silage. Due to their habit of attacking venomous snakes, mongooses have been prized by humans to control rodents and snakes in and around habitations, as made famous in Rudyard Kipling's story of Rikki-tikki-tavi. Hyenas, on the other hand, are often blamed for deaths of both livestock and small children in areas where they come into close contact with humans, and their populations are in decline in both India and Africa outside of protected areas. Among the viverrids, civets are valued for their musk, which is used in perfume, and some African and Indian civets are captured and kept specifically for this purpose.

But without a doubt, the carnivorous species most adapted to human interaction are the domestic dog and cat. Dogs, in particular, have been bred for specialized tasks including hunting, herding, and protection to more than 400 distinct breeds recognized today. Cats, on the other hand, have retained more of their wild instincts and

sloth bear, and sun bear. Giant and lesser pandas have variously been included as members of the bear family or as belonging to the group that includes racoons and their relatives. Scientists still disagree over which classification is correct, as neither panda species is carnivorous. Among bears, the polar bear, with a diet made up of seals and fish, is the only species that feeds exclusively on meat. Most other bears are omnivores, eating fruit, seeds, nuts, and roots as well as meat, fish, and insects.

Bears are generally solitary in habit except during breeding season. Although they do not engage in true hibernation, many species do sleep through much of the winter. Polar bears are currently considered a threatened species due to habitat loss, and grizzly bears, while still numerous in Alaska and Canada, are protected in the continental United States where it is estimated that less than 1,000 remain. Black bears, on the other hand, have become so common in some areas that they are considered nuisance animals, since they easily acclimate to food scraps left in garbage cans and dumps.

The most widespread carnivores are the Canidae, or dog family, which can be found on all continents except Antarctica, although the distinctive dingo of Australia was actually introduced there by early humans many thousands of years ago. The canids include foxes, wolves, jackals, and wild and domestic dogs. They have adapted to environments from the Arctic to the Sahara Desert, and have been domesticated and bred by humans for more than 12,000 years. Most canine species are pack animals. They hunt in cooperative groups and have complex social hierarchies.

Throughout history, wolves have been viewed in a particularly negative light. Children's stories such as *Little Red Riding Hood* and *Peter and the Wolf* perpetuate the myth that the wolf is wanton killer. For thousand of years, wolves have preyed on livestock, but unprovoked attacks on humans are rare. By the middle of the 20th century, gray wolves had been all but exterminated from their territories in the continental United States. They have since been reintroduced to many areas and are now a protected species in the United States and within the provincial parks of Canada. (Canada has a significant wild wolf population outside of the protected areas as well.) Populations in Eurasia are also increasing from former levels, and wolves are protected from hunting in most areas of their range. Two highly endangered species—the red wolf of the southeastern United States and the Abyssinian wolf native to Ethiopia—are also part of this group.

Foxes are among the most diverse of the canid families, with species filling many unique ecological niches. Some examples include the bat-eared fox of southern Africa, the Arctic fox of the northern tundra, and the crab-eating fox of South America—the diet of which actually consists of a variety of small animals, insects, turtle eggs, and birds. Although all are considered foxes, they actually make up several separate genera within the Canid family.

The oldest carnivore family is that of the cat, the body form of which has not changed much since the early Pliocene Epoch, some 5 million years ago. The cat family (Felidae) comprises 37 species that inhabit most of the world, with the exception of Australia and Antarctica. Larger cat species, such as tigers, leopards, lions, and jaguars, are among the most dangerous animals to humans. Some, such as the mountain lion, have become even more menacing as humans increasingly encroach on these animals' territories. However, cats have also been domesticated for thousands of years. Cat domestication dates back at least to the time of the ancient Egyptian civilization. In ancient Egypt, felines were considered sacred

can generally revert to successful survival as a feral animal more easily than dogs. Carnivores in general rank high in intelligence, possessing a large brain in relation to their body size as well as a great ability to learn. Both of these characteristics allow for domestication to come easily to many carnivorous species. In addition to those species that are trained as pets, some carnivores, such as bears and seals, can be trained to perform, whereas others, such as dogs, cheetahs, ferrets, and even otters, can serve as hunting companions.

Clearly, carnivores are a very diverse group of animals, and the various groups may have little in common with one another other than their role as predators. Scientists have had difficulty sorting out all the relationships among and between the various families represented within this order. For example, hyenas were considered to be part of the civet group until fairly recently, and skunks and their relations were at one time included within the weasel family. The aardwolf of South and East Africa looks like a small hyena, but it feeds on termites almost exclusively. The majority of scientists consider it part of the hyena family, but others think it deserves its own separate classification. Most of the existing taxonomy is based more on similarities of structure and function than on the fossil record, but this is changing as more studies using DNA analysis are performed. The relationships among the various families and species will be sorted out in the future. However, the field at present is in flux as scientists evaluate new information and debate the evolutionary importance of each carnivore's physical characteristics.

CHAPTER 1

CARNIVORES

I n a zoological sense, a carnivore is any member of the mammalian order Carnivora (literally, "flesh devourers" in Latin), comprising more than 270 species. In a more general sense, a carnivore is any animal (or plant) that eats other animals, as opposed to a herbivore, which eats plants. Although the species classified in this order are basically meat eaters, a substantial number of them, especially among bears and members of the raccoon family, also feed extensively on vegetation and are thus actually omnivorous.

Snow leopard (Panthera uncia). Russ Kinne/Comstock

The order Carnivora includes 12 families, 9 of which live on land: Canidae (dogs and related species), Felidae (cats), Ursidae (bears), Procyonidae (raccoons and related species), Mustelidae (weasels, badgers, otters, and related species), Mephitidae (skunks and stink badgers), Herpestidae (mongooses), Viverridae (civets, genets, and related species), and Hyaenidae (hyenas). There are three aquatic families: Otariidae (sea lions and fur seals), Phocidae (true, or earless, seals), and Odobenidae (the walrus). These aquatic families are referred to as pinnipeds.

IMPORTANCE OF CARNIVORA

Two carnivores are probably the animals most familiar to people: the domestic dog and cat, both of which are derived from wild members of this order. On the other hand, various bears, felines, canines, and hyenas are among the few animals that occasionally attack humans. These large, dangerous carnivores are often the objects of hunters, who kill them for display as trophies. Most luxurious natural furs (ermine, mink, sable, and otter, among others) come from members of Carnivora, as do many of the animals that attract the largest crowds at circuses and zoos. Producers of livestock worldwide are concerned about possible depredations upon their herds and flocks by this group of mammals.

Being meat eaters, carnivores are at the top of the food chain and form the highest trophic level within ecosystems. As such, they are basic to maintaining the "balance of nature" within those systems. In areas of human settlement, this precarious balance has frequently been upset by the extermination of many carnivores formerly considered undesirable because of their predatory habits. Now, however, carnivores are recognized to be necessary elements

Alaskan Malamute. © Kent & Donna Dannen

in natural systems; they improve the stability of prey populations by keeping them within the carrying capacity of the food supply. As a result, the surviving animals are better fed and less subject to disease. Many of these predators dig dens and provide burrows in which other forms of

Ocicat. © Chanan Photography

wildlife can take refuge. Digging also results in the mixing of soils and the reduction of water runoff during rains. The carnivores best known for their burrow building are badgers and skunks, but bears, canines, and felines regularly engage in this behaviour as well.

Carnivore numbers are limited by food, larger predators, or disease. When human influence removes larger predators, many of the smaller carnivores become extremely abundant, creating an ideal environment for the spread of infection. The disease of most concern to humans is rabies, which is transmitted in saliva via bites. Rabies is most common in the red fox, striped skunk, and

Male lion (Panthera leo). R.I.M. Campbell/Bruce Coleman Ltd.

raccoon, but it also occurs in African hunting dogs and can infect practically all carnivores. Billions of dollars are spent annually throughout the world to manage and control the incidence of this disease. In some countries, abundance of vector species, especially red foxes, is controlled by gathering the animals, or by dropping vaccine-laden bait from the air into their midst. In other countries, programs of "capture-vaccinate-release" are in place to reduce the vulnerability of individual animals. Other infectious diseases carried by carnivores and of concern to humans include canine distemper, parvovirus, toxoplasmosis, and leptospirosis.

Striped skunk (Mephitis mephitis). E.R. Degginger

BEHAVIOUR

Carnivores rank high on the scale of intelligence among mammals. The brain is large in relation to the body, an indication of their superior mental powers. For this reason, these animals are among the easiest to train for entertainment purposes, as pets, or as hunting companions. The highly developed sense of smell among dogs, for instance, supplements the sharper vision of man. Dogs are the carnivores most commonly trained for hunting, but the cheetah, caracal, and ferret have also been used to some extent. In China the otter is trained to drive fish under a large net, which is then dropped and pulled in. Dependent for survival upon their ability to prey upon living animals

Pointer on point. © Sally Anne Thompson/Animal Photography

in a variety of situations, carnivores have evolved a relatively high degree of learning ability.

Carnivorous mammals tend to establish territories, though omnivorous carnivores, such as the black bear, striped skunk, and raccoon, are less apt to do so. Territories are often exclusive, defended by the residents against other animals of their own kind. Such areas may sometimes be marked by secretions produced by anal or other scent glands and by deposition of feces in prominent locations.

There is a wide range of social patterns among carnivores. Many (bears, various foxes, genets, most cats, and most mustelids) are solitary except during the breeding season. Some remain paired throughout the year (black-backed jackal and lesser panda) or occasionally roam in pairs (gray fox, crab-eating fox, and kinkajou). Other carnivores, such as the wolf, African hunting dog, dhole, and coati, normally hunt in packs or bands. Various pinnipeds form sedentary colonies during the breeding season, sea otters congregate during a somewhat larger part of the year, and meerkats are permanently colonial.

Southern sea lions (Otaria byronia). George Holton/Photo Researchers

Mating systems vary among families, ranging from monogamy in the wolf and polygyny in most bears and mustelids to harems in elephant seals. Copulation is vigorous and frequent in many species, including the lion, and many species possess reproductive peculiarities as adaptations to their environments. Induced ovulation, for instance, allows females to release egg cells during or shortly after copulation. Delayed implantation of the fertilized egg in the wall of the uterus is another phenomenon that allows births to occur when resources are abundant. This phenomenon is most prominent in species living in highly seasonal environments. Delayed implantation is most extreme in the pinnipeds and bears but is absent from canines.

FORM AND FUNCTION

The smallest living member of Carnivora is the least weasel (*Mustela nivalis*), which weighs only 25 grams (0.9 ounce). The largest terrestrial form is the Kodiak bear (*Ursus arctos middendorffi*), an Alaskan grizzly bear that is even larger than the polar bear (*Ursus maritimus*). The largest aquatic form is the elephant seal (*Mirounga leonina*), which may weigh 3,700 kg (8,150 pounds). Most carnivores weigh between 4 and 8 kg (9 and 18 pounds).

The vast majority of species are terrestrial, but the pinnipeds are highly adapted to life in the water. Some non-pinnipeds, such as the sea otter, are almost fully aquatic, while others, such as the river otter and polar bear, are semiaquatic, spending most of their lives in or near water. Aquatic and semiaquatic forms have developed specializations such as streamlined bodies and webbed feet.

Carnivores, like other mammals, possess a number of different kinds of teeth: incisors in front, followed by canines, premolars, and molars in the rear. Most carnivores have carnassial, or shearing, teeth that function in slicing meat and cutting tough sinews. The carnassials are usually formed by the fourth upper premolar and the first lower molar, working one against the other with a scissorlike action. Cats, hyenas, and weasels, all highly carnivorous, have well-developed carnassials. Bears and procyonids (except the olingo), which tend to be omnivorous, and seals, which eat fish or marine invertebrates, have little or no modification of these teeth for shearing. The teeth behind the carnassials tend to be lost or reduced in size in highly carnivorous species. Most members of the order have six prominent incisors on both the upper and lower jaw, two canines on each jaw, six to eight premolars, and four molars above and four to six molars below. Incisors are adapted for nipping off flesh. The outermost incisors are usually larger than the inner ones. The strong canines are usually large, pointed, and adapted to aid in the stabbing of prey. The premolars always have sharply pointed cusps, and in some forms (e.g., seals) all the cheek teeth (premolars and molars) have this shape. Except for the carnassials, molars tend to be flat teeth utilized for crushing. Terrestrial carnivores that depend largely on meat tend to have fewer teeth (30 to 34), the flat molars having been lost. Omnivorous carnivores, such as raccoons and bears, have more teeth (40 to 42). Pinnipeds have fewer teeth than terrestrial carnivores. In addition, pinnipeds exhibit little stability in number of teeth; for example, a walrus may have from 18 to 24 teeth.

Several features of the skeleton are characteristic of the order Carnivora. Articulating surfaces (condyles) on the lower jaw form a half-cylindrical hinge that allows the jaw to move only in a vertical plane and with considerable strength. The clavicles (collarbones) are either reduced or absent entirely and, if present, are usually embedded in muscles without articulation with other bones. This allows for a greater flexibility in the shoulder area and prevents breakage of the clavicles when the animal springs on its prey.

The brain is large in relation to the weight of the body, and it contains complex convolutions characteristic of highly intelligent animals. The stomach is simple as opposed to multichambered, and a blind pouch (cecum) attached to the intestine is usually reduced or absent. Since animal tissues are in general simpler to digest than plant tissues, the carnivore's dependence on a diet with a high proportion of meat has led to less-complex compartmentalization of the stomach and a decrease in the length and folding (and therefore surface area) of the intestine. The teats are located on the abdomen along two primitive lines (milk ridges), a characteristic of mammals that lie down when nursing.

Many carnivores have a well-developed penis bone, or baculum. It appears that this structure plays a role in helping to increase the success of copulation and fertilization of eggs in species where numerous males mate with a single female. Cats have a vestigial baculum or none at all, but the baculum of the walrus can measure up to 54 cm (21 inches).

DISTRIBUTION AND ABUNDANCE

Carnivores are found worldwide, although Australia has no native terrestrial members except for the dingo, which was introduced by aboriginal man. Terrestrial forms are naturally absent from most oceanic islands, though the coastlines are usually visited by seals. However, people have taken their pets, as well as a number of wild species, to most islands. For example, a large population of red foxes now inhabits Australia, having been introduced there by foxhunters. Introduction of carnivores to new environments has at times devastated native fauna. In New Zealand, stoats, ferrets, and weasels were introduced to control rabbits, which had also been introduced. As a result, native bird populations were decimated by the carnivores. Birds were also a casualty of mongooses introduced to Hawaii and Fiji, where populations of introduced rodents and snakes had to be controlled. In Europe, American minks released from fur farms contributed to the decline of the native European mink.

North American raccoons (Procyon lotor). Shutterstock.com

Because carnivores are large and depend on meat, there must be fewer carnivores in the environment than the prey animals they feed upon. The maintenance of territories limits the number of predators to the ecosystem's carrying capacity of prey. In general, carnivores have a population density of approximately 1 per 2.5 square km (1 per square mile). By comparison, omnivorous mammals average about 8 per square km (20 per square mile), and herbivorous rodents attain densities of up to 40,000 per square km (100,000 per square mile) at peak population. Relatively low population density makes carnivores vulnerable to fluctuations of prey density, habitat disturbance, infectious disease, and predation by man. The mobility and adaptability of some carnivores has enabled them to shift ecological roles and survive changes brought about by human activities. For example, the red fox, coyote, raccoon, and striped skunk can all be found in urban and suburban areas of North America. In Europe, the red fox lives in most large cities. Most other species do not fare nearly as well. The gray, or timber, wolf and brown bear once lived across much of the Northern Hemisphere, but their ranges have shrunk following habitat destruction, reduction of prey abundance, and persecution as competitors with man. In Africa and southern Asia the same can be said for lions and tigers. Numerous cats and bears and some seals have become rare and are threatened with extinction.

CLASSIFICATION

There is great diversity in Carnivora, especially among the highly specialized pinnipeds. Thus, the characteristics used to separate Carnivora from other mammalian orders and to define the subdivisions of Carnivora are primarily structural. Of great importance are certain features of the skull (such as jaw articulation), feet (number of toes, lack of opposability of the hind toe, type of claws, and fusion of certain bones), and teeth (both the overall tooth pattern and the shape of individual teeth). Dentition is especially important in determining the relationships of fossil forms. Also useful in the taxonomy of modern carnivores are the convolutions around the lateral, or Sylvian, fissure of the brain, the relative weights of the adrenal and thyroid glands, the type of uterus and placenta, and the position of the nipples. Ideally, taxonomy reflects real evolutionary relationships, but in the case of carnivores these must be inferred from a scanty fossil record and from comparisons of modern species. Since there are differences of opinion among specialists as to which taxonomic characteristics should be given priority, there are certain to be alternate classifications, the acceptability of which depends on new information continually being discovered. Undoubtedly, advanced genetic fingerprinting and DNA analyses will allow a more objective classification of species within the order.

As a result of such complicated taxonomic appraisal, the formal classification of Carnivora is in some ways an artificial system set up for the sake of convenience. The major categories of major groups have been in a state of flux for more than a century, and these categories do not seem to be stabilizing, even today. For instance, some mammalogists, tending toward conservative taxonomy, think the relationship of the terrestrial and aquatic carnivores can be best expressed by retaining them in two suborders, the Fissipedia ("split-footed") and Pinnipedia ("feather-footed"), within the single order Carnivora. Most mammalogists at present, however, regard the seals and terrestrial carnivores as belonging to different orders, the Pinnipedia and Carnivora. There are, in reality, only a few features common to the seals and their terrestrial relatives because of the extensive and numerous adaptations the aquatic forms have undergone to make them efficient carnivores of the sea. Mammalogists who have studied seals intensively now realize that there is no anatomical structure unmodified by the extensive aquatic adaptations; every organ and tissue examined has been found to be different in some way from its counterpart in terrestrial forms. This book follows the more modern taxonomic approach, noting similarities between the terrestrial and aquatic groups but focusing mainly on the terrestrial carnivores.

CHAPTER 2

BEARS

A bear (or ursid, being a member of family Ursidae) is any of nine species of large, short-tailed carnivores found in the Americas, Europe, and Asia. The sun bear (*Helarctos malayanus*) is the smallest, often weighing less than 50 kg (110 pounds), and the largest is a subspecies of Alaskan grizzly bear called the Kodiak bear (*Ursus arctos middendorffi*). The polar bear (*Ursus maritimus*), however, is the largest bear species. The black bear (*Ursus americanus*) is common in parts of the United States and Canada.

Giant panda (Ailuropoda melanoleuca) *feeding in a bamboo forest, Sichuan (Szechwan) province, China.* Wolfshead—Ben Osborne/Ardea London

Bears are generally omnivorous, but dietary preferences range from seals for the entirely carnivorous polar bear to assorted vegetation for the largely herbivorous spectacled bear (*Tremarctos ornatus*). The giant panda (*Ailuropoda melanoleuca*) eats only bamboo. Usually gaining weight beforehand, most bears sleep (fitfully) through much of the winter, but they do not truly hibernate. Despite their bulk, most bears climb with ease and swim strongly.

NATURAL HISTORY

Ursids are mainly animals of northern temperate regions and are found farther north than any other mammal. The Arctic fox is found as far north on land, but the polar bear regularly roams on sea ice hundreds of kilometres from shore. Africa and Australia lack bears entirely. The spectacled bear of the South American Andes Mountains is the only species that lives south of the Equator.

Although clumsy in appearance, bears can move surprisingly fast, even through dense cover that would seriously impede a human or a horse. Their senses of sight and hearing, however, are poorly developed, and most hunting is done by smell. Some, such as black and spectacled bears, are strong climbers, and all are strong swimmers, most notably the polar bear. Bears do not generally communicate by sound and usually are quiet, but they do growl at times when feeding, when being challenged by another bear or by humans, and when competing for mates.

Except for the carnivorous polar bear and the vegetarian giant panda, ursids are omnivorous, consuming many items that seem small for an animal of such large size. Ants, bees, seeds of trees, roots, nuts, berries, insect larvae such as grubs, and even the dainty dogtooth violet

Sun bear (Helarctos malayanus). Anthony Mercieca/Root Resources

are eaten. Many bears relish honey, and the sun bear is sometimes called the "honey bear" because of this. Prey taken by bears include rodents, fish, deer, pigs, and seals. Grizzlies (North American subspecies of the brown bear, *Ursus arctos*) are known for their skillful fishing during the spawning runs of salmon. The polar bear's diet is dictated by the Arctic environment, as little vegetation grows within its range. The Asian sloth bear (*Melursus ursinus*) delights especially in raiding and destroying termite nests, sucking up termites and larvae with its funnel-like lips. The giant panda has a special bone formation of the forefoot that functions as a sixth digit; it is opposable to the other five and thus is useful in handling bamboo.

Most bears, including the American and Asiatic black bears (*Ursus americanus* and *U. thibetanus*), eat large amounts of food before entering a den for a period of deep sleep during the winter. The polar bear digs a den in the snow, whereas grizzlies build large mounds of dirt in front of their dens. Bears, however, lack the physiological characteristics (lower heart rate, body temperature, breathing rate, and blood pressure) exhibited by animals that truly hibernate.

Male polar bears sometimes aggregate; otherwise bears are solitary, except during the mating season. Then they tend to congregate, pair off, and mate in seclusion. The male leaves the female soon after mating and plays no role in raising the young. Gestation periods vary, the fertilized egg remaining dormant in the uterus (delayed implantation), which ensures the birth of young while the female is in the winter den and guarantees that the cubs will emerge from the den in the spring, when food is abundant. Ursids breed once per year at most, and many bears breed only every two to four years. The breeding season is usually in late spring or early summer. Delayed implantation results in most births occurring in January

Sloth bear (Melursus ursinus). Bucky Reeves—The National Audubon Society Collection/Photo Researchers

or February. Newborn bears weigh about half a kilogram (one pound) and are about 23 cm (9 inches) long from the nose to the tip of the short tail. Twins are most common in bears, but up to five young may be produced. The cubs nurse for a few months and stay with the female until the next breeding (about a year and a half or more after birth). Most young, however, can get along on their own by about six months of age. Bears reach breeding condition at three and a half to six years of age, males usually maturing later than females. Longevity of bears in the wild ranges from 15 to 30 years, but in captivity they can live considerably longer.

Because of their large size, bears have few natural enemies in the wild. Most mortality occurs because of hunting by humans. On occasion, bears that fail to accumulate enough fat to last throughout the winter may die of starvation. Young bears are more vulnerable to predation because of their smaller size and thus may be killed by other carnivores such as wolves or cougars but most importantly by other bears, especially males. For this reason, females with cubs are highly protective of their young in the vicinity of males.

Home ranges occupied by individual bears vary in size depending on the abundance of food, and larger areas are used when food is in short supply. Although highly variable among geographic areas and even among seasons, American black bears roam areas of 40 to 200 square km (15 to 77 square miles), grizzlies about 300 to 700 square km (115 to 270 square miles). Some polar bears trek across ranges of more than 125,000 square km (48,000 square miles).

FORM AND FUNCTION

In most species, the male is larger than the female. Unlike cats and canids such as dogs and wolves, bears walk in plantigrade fashion (on the soles of their feet with the heels touching the ground) as do humans. Each bear foot has five digits ending in large nonretractile claws that are sometimes adapted for digging, as in the Asian sloth bear. The claws on the front feet are usually better developed than those on the rear, and they are especially adapted for digging out small rodents or nutritious plant roots. The feet generally have hairless soles, but those of the polar bear are covered with hair, enabling the animal to walk on ice with a firm footing. Bears lack a clavicle but have a baculum (penis bone). Their lips are protrusible and mobile. All have a short stubby tail.

Bears have an elongated skull that is especially heavy in the back portion, and their jaws are controlled at the hinge by a powerful set of muscles. The teeth of the omnivorous bears are unspecialized. The first three premolars are usually either missing or extremely small. Except for variability as to the presence of premolars, the ursid dental formula is that of the Carnivora generally, but the sloth bear lacks one pair of upper incisors. The shearing teeth (carnassials) are poorly developed, and the molars have broad, flat crowns.

IMPORTANCE TO HUMANS

If taken when young, bears can be tamed quite easily and are commonly used in circus animal acts. This has often caused people to consider bears as gentle and harmless rather than as potentially dangerous creatures deserving wariness and respect. This mistake has frequently resulted in tragedy for both humans and bears. Grizzly and polar bears are the most dangerous, but Eurasian brown bears and American black bears have also been known to attack humans. Some species depredate livestock on occasion, and some ursids, such as Asiatic and American black bears, may destroy fruit or other crops, especially corn.

The pelts of bears have been used for a number of purposes. Perhaps most popular has been the bearskin rug. Skins also have been used for fashionable articles of clothing. The meat of black and polar bears often is consumed. The teeth and claws of bears have been favourite ornaments among Native American peoples, and the fat furnishes "bear grease," which is used for cooking. The gall bladders of Asian bears are greatly valued in Asia for pharmaceutical purposes.

EVOLUTION

The bear family is the most recently evolved lineage of carnivores. Its ancestral line appears to have diverged from canid stock during the Late Miocene Epoch and to have developed into modern species through such Pliocene forms as *Hyaenarctos* of Europe, Asia, and North America. The red, or lesser, panda (*Ailurus fulgens*) is also classified as a bear, though along with the giant panda it is sometimes classified in a separate family, Ailuridae.

FAMILIAR BEARS

Because of their size and power, bears have long fascinated the general public. Ethologists, too, are fascinated by the range of behaviours demonstrated by members of Ursidae, from the solitary and retiring and almost completely vegetarian giant panda to the equally solitary but utterly fearless and carnivorous polar bear.

AMERICAN BLACK BEARS

The American black bear (*Ursus americanus*), or simply black bear, is the most common bear. It is found in the

30 centimeters
12 inches

American Black Bear
(*Ursus americanus*)

Many black bears are indeed black, but others have blue-gray, reddish-brown, or even white fur. In western North America, this species is commonly brown.
Encyclopædia Britannica, Inc.

forests of North America, including parts of Mexico. The American black bear consists of only one species, but its colour varies, even among members of the same litter. White markings may occur on the chest, sometimes in the shape of a V. Depending on their colour variations, black bears are often referred to as cinnamon bears, blue-gray or blue-black glacier bears, and white bears (found mainly on Princess Royal Island, British Columbia). Black bears that are actually brown in colour are most common in western North America. They are sometimes called brown bears, but the true brown bear (*Ursus arctos*; also called the grizzly bear in North America) is much larger.

The black bear is large and stocky and has a short tail. Adults range from 1.5 to 1.8 metres (5 to 6 feet) in length and weigh 90 to 270 kg (200 to 600 pounds). Males can be up to 70 percent heavier than females. The head is small but is supported by a strong neck. The ears are small and rounded. The curved claws are nonretractile, and, unlike cats and dogs, bears walk on the soles of their feet in plantigrade locomotion.

Though classified as carnivores, black bears have an omnivorous diet. In spring they consume emerging plants and carcasses of animals that have died during the winter. Fruits dominate the diet in summer, and both fruit and mast, especially acorns and beechnuts, constitute most of the fall diet. As opportunistic feeders, black bears will also eat pinecones, roots, ants, and honey from wild or domestic bees. Nonetheless, black bears are strong predators, and in some areas they frequently kill moose calves and deer fawns during spring. Black bears living near humans adapt readily to alternate food sources, such as garbage from dumps or campsites and handouts from tourists in parks. Human encounters with black bears occasionally result in injury or death, and attacks are reported every year. In almost all cases, avoiding surprise encounters is the best defense, as black bears prefer to stay away from people.

Throughout most of their range, black bears become dormant during winter. They spend the winter in dens located in rock crevices, in underground burrows, under tree roots, in hollow trees, in brush piles, or simply on open-ground beds. Prior to winter sleep, bears must accumulate large quantities of body fat during late summer and fall. Not only does this enable them to survive the long period of winter fasting, but it also allows them to have sufficient energy in spring when they emerge and food is rare. For females, the amount of fat stored before winter is linked with reproductive success: fatter females typically have more and bigger young than do leaner females. Accumulating fat for the winter is thus a strong drive, and it explains the constant search for food through the summer and fall.

Black bears are not territorial; they are mostly solitary, and the home ranges of both males and females may overlap. Home ranges typically are larger where food is less abundant and smaller where food is plentiful. Throughout Canada and the United States, home ranges of black bears extend from about 40 to 200 square km (15 to 77 square miles) for males but are considerably smaller for females. Breeding begins in the spring and peaks during June and July. Black bears are promiscuous, males and females often mating with several individuals. Implantation of the fertilized egg is delayed, occurring in November or December. Actual gestation then lasts 60 to 70 days, and one to four young cubs are born in January or February. Born blind, fully furred, and toothless, the cubs remain with the mother for 16 months, and

A squirrel-proof bird feeder is no match for this adolescent black bear, an unexpected visitor to a backyard southeast of Buffalo, N.Y. Tyrone Georgiou

the female breeds every second or third year. Although the mother is very protective of her litter, young cubs may be killed by coyotes, wolves, brown bears, or other black bears. Black bears can live for more than 20 years in the wild, but in areas near human habitation most black bears die sooner as a result of hunting, trapping, poaching, nuisance removal near campgrounds or dumps, and collision with vehicles.

In natural habitats, black bears are active during the day, but in areas of high human activity such as dumps and campsites, black bears often become nocturnal to avoid encounters with humans. Even so, black bears habituate quickly to handouts given by tourists, and this lack of fear of humans often leads to conflicts. In parks, human-habituated bears often must be killed as they become hazardous around campsites. Not feeding wild black bears is therefore better for both humans and bears. However, as an animal capable of being tamed and taught various tricks, the black bear is a common performer in circuses and other animal acts.

ASIATIC BLACK BEARS

The Asiatic black bear (*Ursus thibetanus*), also called the Himalayan bear, Tibetan bear, or moon bear, is found in the Himalayas, Southeast Asia, and part of eastern Asia, including Japan. The Asiatic black bear is omnivorous, eating insects, fruit, nuts, beehives, small mammals, and birds, as well as carrion. It will occasionally attack domestic animals. It is similar to the American black bear in size and appearance. It has a glossy black (sometimes brownish) coat, with a whitish mark shaped like a crescent moon on the chest. Its long, coarse neck and shoulder hair forms a modified mane. The Ainu people of

Asiatic Black Bear
(*Ursus thibetanus*)

30 centimeters
12 inches

Ursus thibetanus, found in the forests of Asia, has a black or brownish coat with a whitish mark shaped like a crescent moon on the chest. For this reason, it is sometimes called the moon bear. Encyclopædia Britannica, Inc.

Japan worship the bear as a god of the mountains and as an ancestor of some mountain-dwelling Ainu. The bear's gall bladder and bile are highly valued for use in traditional Asian medicines, especially in Japan, South Korea, and Singapore. In China, bile is "farmed" by extracting it from captive bears, but elsewhere in Asia wild bears are hunted for their gall bladders and other body parts.

During the summer the Asiatic black bear lives mainly in forested hills and mountains at elevations up to 3,600 metres (11,800 feet). Becoming fat by fall, it spends the winter at elevations of 1,500 metres (5,000 feet) or less and may sleep for much of the time. An adult male weighs 100 to 200 kg (220 to 440 pounds), a female about half as much; its length averages about 130 to 190 cm (51 to 75 inches), in addition to a 7- to 10-cm (3- to 4-inch) tail. After weaning, the young remain with the mother for as long as three years.

BROWN BEARS

The brown bear (*Ursus arctos*) is a shaggy-haired bear native to Europe, Asia, and northwestern North America. More than 80 forms of brown bear have been described; they are treated as several subspecies of *Ursus arctos*. North American brown bears are traditionally called grizzlies.

Eurasian brown bears are generally solitary animals that are able to run and swim well. They are usually 120 to 210 cm (48 to 84 inches) long and weigh 135 to 250 kg (300 to 550 pounds). The exceptionally large Siberian brown bear (*Ursus arctos beringianus*), weighing as much as 360 kg (800 pounds), approximates the size of the North American grizzly. Eurasian brown bears feed on mammals, fish, and plant material. Coat colour is highly variable, ranging from grayish white through bluish and brownish shades to almost black. Eurasian brown bears are commonly seen in zoos; formerly they were often trained to move rhythmically to music—the so-called dancing bears of European carnivals and festivals. They originally roamed most of Europe and Asia, and, though perhaps 100,000 remain in northern Eurasia, the southern range has been significantly reduced.

Brown bears are omnivorous and feed on berries, plant roots and shoots, small mammals, fish, calves of many hoofed animals, and carrion. They often cache food in shallow holes, and they dig readily and strongly in search of rodents. Except in some southern areas, bears retire to dens in winter and therefore accumulate

Brown Bear
(*Ursus arctos*)

30 centimeters
12 inches

Brown bears can be fierce and are strong enough to carry off small horses and cattle. Encyclopædia Britannica, Inc.

large amounts of fat during late summer and autumn. Cubs, usually twins, are born in winter after about 6 to 8 months of gestation. At birth a cub weighs less than a kilogram (2.2 pounds).

GRIZZLY BEARS

Grizzly bear is a traditional name given to brown bears (*Ursus arctos*) of North America. Grizzly bears of the northern Rocky Mountains (*U. arctos horribilis*) are classified as a subspecies, as are the huge Kodiak bears (*U. arctos middendorffi*) of Alaska.

Grizzlies are massive animals with humped shoulders and an elevated forehead that contributes to a somewhat concave profile. The fur is brownish to buff, and the hairs are usually silver- or pale-tipped to give the grizzled effect for which they are named. Large adult grizzlies may be about 2.5 metres (8 feet) long and weigh about 410 kg (900 pounds). The Kodiak bear, which lives only on Kodiak Island and neighbouring islands, is the largest living land carnivore and may attain a length of more than 3 metres and a weight of 780 kg. Because of their bulk and long, straight claws, these bears rarely climb even as cubs. Other grizzlies, however, are surprisingly agile and can run as fast as 48 km per hour (30 mph). Their eyesight is poor, and they have been known to attack humans without evident provocation. Females with cubs are the most aggressive.

Omnivorous animals, grizzlies feed on berries, plant roots and shoots, small mammals, fish, calves of many hoofed animals, and carrion. Food is often cached in shallow holes, and grizzlies dig readily and vigorously in search of rodents. Each spring the bear marks the boundary of its territory by rubbing trees, scratching bark, or even biting large pieces from the trunks of trees. During late summer and autumn, grizzlies accumulate large amounts of fat and then retire to dens in winter. Cubs, most often twins, are usually born in January or February after about 6 to 8 months of gestation.

Grizzlies once ranged through forested and open regions of western North America from Alaska to Mexico. Formerly living across the Great Plains, the grizzly bear has been the subject of many Native American legends and

Giant Panda
(*Ailuropoda melanoleuca*)

30 centimeters
12 inches

The giant panda (Ailuropoda melanoleuca) of China was long thought to be very closely related to raccoons, but it is now widely classified as a bear. Encyclopædia Britannica, Inc.

was one of the mammals reported by Lewis and Clark in their journey through eastern Montana in 1804. Grizzlies remain numerous in Alaska and Canada, where they continue to be highly prized as big game. In the continental United States, however, less than 1,000 remain, and they are protected by law.

The American black bear (*Ursus americanus*) is sometimes mistaken for the grizzly because it is sometimes brown in western parts of its range.

GIANT PANDAS

The giant panda (*Ailuropoda melanoleuca*), also called the panda bear, is a bearlike mammal inhabiting bamboo forests in the mountains of central China. Its striking coat of black and white, combined with a bulky body and round face, gives it a captivating appearance that has endeared it to people worldwide. According to the International Union for Conservation of Nature (IUCN) Red List of Threatened Species, fewer than 2,500 mature pandas are thought to remain in the wild.

Large males may attain 1.8 metres (6 feet) in length and weigh more than 100 kg (220 pounds); females are usually smaller. Round black ears and black eye patches stand out against a white face and neck. Black limbs, tail, legs, and shoulders contrast with the white torso. The rear paws point inward, which gives pandas a waddling gait. Pandas can easily stand on their hind legs and are commonly observed somersaulting, rolling, and dust-bathing. Although somewhat awkward as climbers, pandas readily ascend trees and, on the basis of their resemblance to bears, are probably capable of swimming. An unusual anatomic characteristic is an enlarged wrist bone that functions somewhat like a thumb, enabling pandas to handle food with considerable dexterity.

NATURAL HISTORY

As much as 90 to 98 percent of the panda's diet consists of the leaves, shoots, and stems of bamboo, a large grass available year-round in much of China's forested regions. Despite adaptations in the forepaws, teeth, and jaws for bamboo consumption, the giant panda has retained the digestive system of its carnivore ancestry and is therefore unable to digest cellulose, a main constituent of bamboo. Pandas solve this problem by rapidly passing prodigious quantities of the grass through their digestive tracts on a daily basis. As much as 16 out of every 24 hours is spent feeding, and elimination of wastes occurs up to 50 times per day. Fossilized dental remains indicate that the giant panda committed to bamboo as its principal food source at least three million years ago. Although unable to capture prey, pandas retain a taste for meat, which is used as bait to capture them for radio collaring and has made them pests in human camps on occasion. The species cannot naturally survive outside bamboo forests, though in captivity they have been maintained on cereals, milk, and garden fruits and vegetables. Bamboo is the healthier diet for captive pandas.

The giant panda's solitary nature is underscored by its reliance on its sense of smell (olfaction). Each animal confines its activities to a range of about 4 to 6 square km (1.5 to 2.3 square miles), but these home ranges often overlap substantially. Under this arrangement scent functions in regulating contact between individuals. A large scent gland located just below the tail and surrounding the anus is used to leave olfactory messages for other pandas. The gland is rubbed against trees, rocks, and clumps of grass, with scent conveying information on identity, sex, and possibly social status of the marking individual. Chemical analysis of marks is consistent with a difference in function for males and females. Males appear to use scent to identify the areas where they live, whereas females primarily use it for signaling estrus (heat). Except for the mothers' care of infants, the only social activity of pandas takes place during females' estrus, which occurs annually during the spring and lasts one to three days. A spring mating season (March to May) and a fall birth season (August to September) are seen in both wild and captive populations. Males appear to locate females first by scent and ultimately by vocalizations. Assemblages of one to five males per female have been recorded. At this time males may become highly aggressive as they compete for the opportunity to mate.

Like bears, giant pandas undergo a delay in implantation of the fertilized ovum into the wall of the uterus, a period of two to three months after mating. Hormone levels in females' urine indicate that the period of embryonic/fetal growth and development lasts only about two months. Altogether, gestation averages 135 days (with a range of 90 to 184 days), but, because of the short growth phase, a term fetus weighs only about 112 grams (4 ounces) on average. Relative to the mother, giant pandas produce the smallest offspring of any placental mammal (about 1/800 of the mother's weight). For the first two to three weeks of life, the mother uses her forepaws and her thumblike wrist bones to cuddle and position the infant against herself in a rather uncarnivore-like and almost human fashion. Nearly half of the 133 captive births recorded before 1998 were of twins, but panda mothers are typically unable to care for more than one infant. Reasons for the extremely small size of the offspring and the frequent production of twins are not understood, but both are traits shared with bears.

The newborn panda is blind and covered with only a thin all-white coat. It is virtually helpless, being able only to suckle and vocalize. It depends on its mother for warmth, nourishment, positioning at the breast, and stimulating the passage of wastes. Development is slow during the early months. Eyes begin to open at about 45 days, and the first wobbly steps are taken at 75 to 80 days. Its helpless state mandates birth in a den, an environment in which it lives for the first 100 to 120 days of life. By about 14 months, at which age the milk teeth have erupted, the infant readily consumes bamboo, and at 18 to 24 months weaning from the mother takes place. Separation from the mother must occur before a female can undertake the production of her next litter. Captive pandas may live beyond 30 years in captivity, but life span in the wild is estimated at about 20 years.

CONSERVATION AND CLASSIFICATION

Fossils from northern Myanmar (Burma) and Vietnam and much of China as far north as Beijing indicate that the giant panda was widely distributed throughout eastern Asia during the early Pleistocene Epoch (2.6 million to 11,700 years ago). Human destruction of its forest habitat, combined with poaching, has restricted the species to remote fragments of mountain habitat along the eastern edge of the Tibetan Plateau in the Chinese provinces of Sichuan (Szechwan), Shaanxi (Shensi), and Gansu (Kansu). The total area of these habitats is about 13,000 square km (5,000 square miles), and in recent times periodic mass flowering and die-offs of bamboo have brought starvation for some populations. (Five to 10 years are required for bamboo forests to recover from these natural events.) Since the 1990s China has greatly expanded its conservation efforts, and it now regards this endangered species as a national treasure. The reserve system has been expanded from 14 sites to more than 40, and cooperative international arrangements were implemented to provide training in reserve management and captive breeding. Prior eras of giving pandas as gifts and

LESSER PANDAS

The lesser panda (*Ailurus fulgens*), also called the red panda, cat bear, bear cat, or red bear cat, is a reddish brown, long-tailed, raccoonlike mammal, about the size of a large cat, that is found in the mountain forests of the Himalayas and adjacent areas of eastern Asia. It subsists mainly on bamboo and other vegetation, fruits, and insects. Like its possible relative the giant panda, the lesser panda has been classified as a member of the raccoon family (Procyonidae), the bear family (Ursidae), and an entirely separate family (Ailuridae).

The lesser panda has soft, thick fur—rich reddish brown above and black underneath. The face is white, with a stripe of red-brown from each eye to the corners of the mouth; and the bushy tail is faintly ringed. The head and body length of the lesser panda is 50 to 65 cm (20 to 26 inches); the tail is 30 to 50 cm (12 to 20 inches) long; and the weight ranges from 3 to 4.5 kg (6.5 to 10 pounds). The feet have hairy soles, and the claws are semiretractile.

The lesser panda lives high in the mountains among rocks and trees and climbs with agility (though its tail is not prehensile). It seems to do most of its feeding on the ground. It is nocturnal and may live alone, in pairs, or in family groups. The litters generally contain one or two young that are born in spring after a gestation period of about 130 days. The animal is gentle and easily tamed but usually resents being handled. It is a very popular zoo animal and is frequently involved in the animal trade.

of short-term commercial loans to zoos have given way to lending agreements that generate funds for preservation of the wild population. More than 120 pandas are maintained in captivity in China, and another 15 to 20 are found in zoos elsewhere. Captive populations are increasing. Su-Lin, the first of the giant pandas to be exhibited in the West, reached the United States as an infant in 1936 and was a popular attraction at the Brookfield Zoo, near Chicago, until its death in 1938. No European observed a live giant panda in the wild until the Walter Stötzner expedition of 1913–15, although Armand David, a Jesuit missionary, discovered some panda furs in 1869.

The classification of giant pandas has long been a subject of controversy. Anatomic, behavioral, and biochemical data have been used to place pandas with bears (family Ursidae), with raccoons (Procyonidae), or in a completely separate family (Ailuridae). Improved molecular analyses made during the 1990s strongly suggest bears as the giant panda's closest relatives, and many of their behavioral and reproductive characteristics are consistent with this placement.

POLAR BEARS

The polar bear (*Ursus maritimus*), also called the white bear, sea bear, or ice bear, is a great white northern bear found throughout the Arctic region. The polar bear travels long

30 centimeters
12 inches

Polar Bear
(*Ursus maritimus*)

The polar bear is about as large and potentially dangerous as the brown bear. Encyclopædia Britannica, Inc.

distances over vast desolate expanses, generally on drifting oceanic ice floes, searching for seals, its primary prey. Except for one subspecies of grizzly bear, the polar bear is the largest and most powerful carnivore on land. It has no natural predators and knows no fear of humans, making it an extremely dangerous animal.

Polar bears are stocky, with a long neck, relatively small head, short, rounded ears, and a short tail. The male, which is much larger than the female, weighs 410 to 720 kg (900 to 1,600 pounds). It grows to about 1.6 metres (5.3 feet) tall at the shoulder and 2.2 to 2.5 metres in length. The tail is 7 to 12 cm (3 to 5 inches) long. Sunlight can pass through the thick fur, its heat being absorbed by the bear's black skin. Under the skin is a layer of insulating fat. The broad feet have hairy soles to protect and insulate as well as to facilitate movement across ice, as does the uneven skin on the soles of the feet, which helps to prevent slipping. Strong, sharp claws are also important for gaining traction, for digging through ice, and for killing prey.

Polar bears are solitary and strictly carnivorous, feeding especially on the ringed seal but also on the bearded seal and other pinnipeds. The bear stalks seals resting on the ice, ambushes them near breathing holes, and digs young seals from snow shelters where they are born. Polar bears prefer ice that is subject to periodic fracturing by wind and sea currents, because these fractures offer seals access to both air and water. As their prey is aquatic, polars bears are excellent swimmers, and they are even known to kill beluga whales. In swimming the polar bear uses only its front limbs, an aquatic adaptation found in no other four-legged mammal. Polar bears are opportunistic as well as predatory; they will consume dead fish and carcasses of stranded whales and eat garbage near human settlements.

Mating occurs in spring, and implantation of the fertilized ovum is delayed. Including the delay, gestation may last 195 to 265 days, and one to four cubs, usually two, are born during the winter in a den of ice or snow. Cubs weigh less than 1 kg (2.2 pounds) at birth and are not weaned until after they are two years old. Young polar bears may die of starvation or may be killed by adult males, and for this reason female polar bears are extremely defensive of their young when adult males are present. Young remain with their mothers until they reach sexual maturity. Females first reproduce at four to eight years of age and breed every two to four years thereafter. Males mature at about the same age as females but do not breed until a few years later. Adult polar bears have no natural predators, though walruses and wolves can kill them. Longevity in the wild is 25 to 30 years, but in captivity several polar bears have lived to more than 35 years old.

Humans probably cause most polar bear deaths by hunting and by destruction of problem animals near settlements. Polar bears have been known to kill people. The bears are hunted especially by Inuit people for their hides, tendons, fat, and flesh. Although polar bear meat is consumed by aboriginals, the liver is inedible and often poisonous because of its high vitamin A content.

At the turn of the 21st century, an estimated 20,000 to 25,000 polar bears existed in the wild. Because of continued global warming, a substantial reduction in the coverage of Arctic summer sea ice—prime habitat for polar bears—is expected by the middle of the 21st century. Models developed by some scientists predict an increase in polar bear starvation as a result of longer ice-free seasons and a decline in mating success, since sea-ice fragmentation could reduce encounter rates between males and females. Model forecasts by the U.S. Geological

Survey suggest that habitat loss may cause polar bear populations to decline by two-thirds by the year 2050. In May 2008 the U.S. government listed the polar bear as a threatened species.

SLOTH BEARS

The sloth bear (*Melursus ursinus*), also called the honey bear (in Hindi, *bhalu*), is a forest-dwelling ursid that inhabits tropical or subtropical regions of India and Sri Lanka. Named for its slow-moving habits, the sloth bear has poor senses of sight and hearing but does have a good sense of smell. Various adaptations equip this nocturnal

Sloth Bear
(*Melursus ursinus*)

30 centimeters
12 inches

The shaggy sloth bear, which lives in India, Sri Lanka, and other parts of South Asia sucks up insects and larvae with its funnel-like lips. Encyclopædia Britannica, Inc.

animal for raiding insect colonies. With long, curved front claws (extending from large paws), it digs toward and rips open a nest of bees or termites. Inserting its long snout into the nest and closing its nostrils (thereby preventing entry of insects into its respiratory passages), the sloth bear opens its protrusible lips and sucks in the insects through the gap caused by the lack of central upper incisors. Supplements to this diet include fruit, honey, grains, and small vertebrates.

An adult usually stands about 75 cm (30 inches) at the shoulder, weighs 91 to 113 kg (200 to 250 pounds), and is about 1.5 metres (5 feet) long, with a 7- to 12-cm (3- to 5-inch) tail. Shades of gray, red, or brown may tinge its black, shaggy coat, composed of long hairs—longest between the shoulders. Whitish to yellowish coloured hair marks its snout and forms a crescent or chevron on its chest.

Following the normal gestation period of seven months, the female bears a litter of one to three cubs. Reportedly remaining with her two to three years, these cubs often ride around on their mother's back.

SPECTACLED BEARS

The spectacled bear (*Tremarctos ornatus*), also called the Andean bear, is the only South American species of the family Ursidae. It inhabits mountainous regions (particularly of the Andes), dwelling primarily in forested areas, and it feeds mainly on shoots and fruit.

The spectacled bear is an agile climber. The adult stands to 64 cm (about 25 inches) at the shoulder and varies from 1.2 to 1.8 metres (4 to 6 feet) in length, with a 7-cm (3-inch) tail. Its shaggy coat varies from dark brown to black. Characteristic whitish to yellowish marks usually encircle the eyes partially or completely to form

Spectacled Bear
(*Tremarctos ornatus*)

30 centimeters
12 inches

The southernmost ursid, the spectacled bear is the only bear found in South America. Encyclopædia Britannica, Inc.

"spectacles," often extending down the neck and to the chest. Litters of one to three cubs have been born in captivity after a gestation period of 8 to 8½ months.

SUN BEARS

The sun bear (*Helarctos*, or *Ursus*, *malayanus*), also called the bruang, honey bear, or Malayan sun bear, is the smallest member of the family Ursidae, found in Southeast Asian forests. The bear is often tamed as a pet when young but becomes bad-tempered and dangerous as an adult. It weighs only 27 to 65 kg (59 to 143 pounds) and grows 1 to 1.2 metres (3.3 to 4 feet) long with a 5-cm (2-inch) tail. Its large forepaws bear long, curved claws, which it uses for tearing or digging in its search for insect nests and colonies, particularly those of bees and termites. Other items

Sun Bear
(*Helarctos malayanus*)

30 centimeters
12 inches

The sun bear's extremely long tongue is well suited for lapping up insects and honey. Encyclopædia Britannica, Inc.

of its omnivorous diet include fruit, honey, and small vertebrates.

Generally nocturnal, the tree-climbing sun bear is shy and retiring but quite intelligent. It has an orange-yellow-coloured chest crescent that according to legend represents the rising sun. Other light features (often including its muzzle and feet) contrast with its black coat of short, coarse fur.

CHAPTER 3
CANINES

A canine, or canid, is any of 34 living species of foxes, wolves, jackals, and other members of the dog family, Canidae. Found throughout the world, canines tend to be slender, long-legged animals with long muzzles, bushy tails, and erect, pointed ears.

Canines are carnivores that prey on a wide variety of animals, large and small, though some also eat carrion and vegetable matter. Highly intelligent and easily trained,

Siberian husky. © Sally Anne Thompson/Animal Photography

canines were probably the first animals to be domesticated. On the other hand, most species have been (and are still) hunted for their pelts, and in many areas they continue to be hunted, trapped, and otherwise controlled in order to mitigate predation on livestock and game.

NATURAL HISTORY

Each continent except Antarctica and Australia has members of the family Canidae native to it; Australia's dingo (*Canis dingo*, *Canis lupus dingo*, or *Canis lupus familiaris dingo*) was introduced by man, albeit thousands of years ago. Native canines are absent from New Zealand and most oceanic islands. Every major ecosystem is inhabited by some type of canine. The Arctic fox (*Alopex lagopus*), for example, occupies the barren tundra of the Arctic,

Bush dog (Speothos venaticus). Richard Batchelor/EB Inc.

whereas the fennec (*Vulpes zerda*) lives in the Sahara desert. In general, however, canines tend to be animals of open or grassland areas. The rare bush dog (*Speothos venaticus*) of South America confines itself to forests and wet savannas, however, and the Eurasian raccoon dog (*Nyctereutes procyonoides*) often lives in tree hollows that have their entrances close to the ground. The American gray fox (*Urocyon cinereoargenteus*) prefers wooded areas and is not averse to climbing trees, whereas the red fox (*Vulpes vulpes*) tends to occupy meadows and farmland. Thus, in North America, where both these foxes exist, they occupy slightly different ecological niches.

Canines are all predators that are primarily, if not exclusively, meat eaters. The gray, or timber, wolf (*Canis lupus*), the African hunting dog (*Lycaon pictus*), and the Asian dhole (*Cuon alpinus*) are strictly carnivorous, whereas foxes, jackals, the coyote (*Canis latrans*), and the raccoon dog eat fruits and berries as well as small mammals, birds, insects, crustaceans, and mollusks. The vision and hearing of canines are acute, and their sense of smell is among the keenest of all mammals. The canines that are strictly carnivorous tend to hunt in packs; those that are omnivorous tend to be solitary in their hunting habits. Carnivorous species usually follow migratory herds of hoofed animals such as caribou or antelope, or they move into areas where other prey is more numerous. African hunting dogs are extremely social, always hunting in intricately organized packs, whereas the varied diet of omnivores reduces the necessity for organized attack and extended travel to such an extent that some South American foxes are solitary or live in pairs.

Canine litters usually number about four to six young born after a gestation period of 51 to 80 days, depending on the species. The Arctic fox has the largest litter among

DOMINANCE HIERARCHY

Dominance hierarchy is a form of animal social structure in which a linear or nearly linear ranking exists, with each animal dominant over those below it and submissive to those above it in the hierarchy. Dominance hierarchies are best known in social mammals, such as baboons and wolves, and in birds, notably chickens (in which the term pecking order or peck right is often applied).

In most cases the dominance hierarchy is relatively stable from day to day. Direct conflict is rare; an animal usually steps aside when confronted by one of higher rank. Temporary shifts occur; for instance, a female baboon mated to a high-ranking male assumes a high rank for the duration of the pair-bond. An individual weakened by injury, disease, or senility usually moves downward in rank.

carnivores, averaging about 11 but sometimes numbering 20 or more. Arctic foxes give birth in a den in the ground, in a hollow log or tree, in a hidden brushy area, among boulders, or in a crevice of rock. The African hunting dog often dens in abandoned aardvark burrows. Canines breed in late winter, and the young are born in mid- or late spring. Their eyes usually open in about two weeks, and they nurse for four to six weeks. The smaller species can begin breeding when only one year old, but larger forms, such as the wolf, do not reach sexual maturity until two or three years of age.

Canines communicate with a variety of sounds. The vocal repertoire is most highly developed in social species and includes howls, yelps, snarls, barks, and growls. These sounds are frequently associated with specialized visual signals involving movements of the ears and tail, raising of certain areas of fur, and baring of teeth. Within the social group or pack there is a complex dominance hierarchy based on age, pair-bonds, physical condition, and sexual state. Vocal and visual signals serve to minimize aggressive interactions, such as quarrels over food, that might prove injurious. In solitary species, vocalizations serve to advertise territory, ward off aggressors, and communicate with the mate and young.

FORM AND FUNCTION

A long face or muzzle is characteristic of wild canines. All have a relatively long and bushy tail. Most have a uniform coloration, although there are some contrasting colours on jackals and the gray fox, a dark mask on the raccoon dog, a blotching of black, yellow, and white on the African hunting dog, and a lighter-coloured belly in most species. The ears are pointed, erect, and often quite large in desert species. In addition to detecting sound, large ears are believed to act as heat regulators in species such as the

Fennec (Fennecus zerda). Anthony Mercieca—The National Audubon Society Collection/Photo Researchers

bat-eared fox (*Otocyon megalotis*) and the fennec, allowing a greater amount of heat to be dissipated in hot climates. Arctic foxes tend to have much smaller ears, providing less loss of heat in a region where heat conservation is important to survival.

Most canines have relatively long legs, especially the maned wolf (*Chrysocyon brachyurus*) of South America. This feature makes canines well-adapted to running, as does the fact that they walk on their toes (digitigrade locomotion). Canines have exceptional stamina but are not capable of great bursts of speed. During winter, northern species often grow fur on their foot pads to provide traction on snow and protection from the cold.

Maned wolf (Chrysocyon brachyurus). Kenneth W. Fink/Root Resources

remained only in the northeastern corner of Minnesota. In the late 20th century, greater tolerance, legal protection, and other factors allowed their range to expand in portions of North America and Europe.

Wolves are probably more popular now than at any other time in recorded history. In 1995 wolves from Canada were reintroduced to Yellowstone National Park and Idaho, and captive-reared Mexican wolves (a subspecies) were released to their former range in eastern Arizona beginning in 1998. At the beginning of the 21st century, an estimated 65,000 to 78,000 wolves inhabited North America. Canada had the largest population (although the provinces of New Brunswick, Nova Scotia, and Prince Edward Island had no wolves), followed by Alaska and Minnesota. Some of the western states as well as Michigan and Wisconsin have smaller but recovering wolf populations. Canadian wolves are protected only within provincial parks, whereas all wolves in the contiguous United States receive some level of legal protection by federal and state governments. Populations in southern Europe and Scandinavia are relatively small but are increasing. The Eurasian population probably exceeds 150,000 and is stable or increasing in most countries, and most afford the wolf some degree of legal protection. Worldwide, wolves still occupy about two-thirds of their former range. Although often thought of as wilderness animals, wolves can and do thrive close to people when they are not excessively persecuted and food is available.

Wolves usually live in packs of up to two dozen individuals, but packs numbering 6 to 10 are most common. A pack is basically a family group consisting of an adult breeding pair (the alpha male and alpha female) and their offspring of various ages. Each individual has its own distinct personality. The ability of wolves to form strong social bonds with one another is what makes the wolf pack possible. A dominance hierarchy is established within the pack, which helps maintain order. The alpha male and female continually assert themselves over their subordinates, and they guide the activities of the group. The female predominates in roles such as care and defense of pups, whereas the male predominates in foraging and food provisioning and in travels associated with those activities. Both sexes are very active in attacking and killing prey, but during the summer hunts are often conducted alone.

A pack's territory can be 80 to 3,000 square km (31 to 1,200 square miles), depending on prey abundance, and it is vigorously defended against neighbouring packs. Wolves communicate with one another by visual signaling (facial expression, body position, tail position), vocalizations, and scent marking. Howling helps the pack stay in contact and also seems to strengthen social bonds among pack members. Along with howling, marking of territory with urine and feces lets neighbouring packs know they should not intrude. Intruders are often killed by resident packs, yet in some circumstances they are accepted.

Breeding occurs between February and April, and a litter of usually five or six pups is born in the spring after a gestation period of about two months. The young are usually born in a den consisting of a natural hole or a burrow, often in a hillside. A rock crevice, hollow log, overturned stump, or abandoned beaver lodge may be used as a den, and even a depression beneath the lower branches of a conifer will sometimes suffice. All members of the pack care solicitously for the young. After being weaned from their mother's milk at six to nine weeks, they are fed a diet of regurgitated meat. Throughout spring and summer the pups are the centre of attention as well as the geographic focus of the pack's activities. After a few weeks pups are usually moved from the den to a "rendezvous site" above ground where they play and sleep while adults hunt. The pups grow rapidly and are moved farther and more often as summer comes to an end. In autumn the pack starts to travel again within its territory, and the pups must keep up. Most pups are almost adult size by October or November. After two or more years in the pack, many leave to search for a mate, establish a new territory, and possibly even start their own pack. Those who stay with the pack may eventually replace a parent to become a breeding animal (alpha). Large packs seem to result from fewer young wolves' leaving the group and from litters' being produced by more than one female. Wolves that leave their packs are known to have traveled as far as 886 km (550 miles).

Wolves are renowned for their wide-ranging travels, and it is not unusual for them to cover 20 km (12 miles) or more in a day. They move and hunt mostly at night, especially in areas populated by humans and during warm weather. The main prey are large herbivores such as deer, elk, moose, bison, bighorn sheep, caribou, and musk oxen, which they chase, seize, and pull to the ground. Beavers and hares are eaten when available, and wolves in western Canada even fish for Pacific salmon. A large percentage of the animals that wolves kill are young, old, or in poor condition. After making a kill, the pack gorges (consuming some 3 to 9 kg [7 to 20 pounds] per animal) and then lingers, often reducing the carcass to hair and a few bones before moving on to look for another meal.

Biologists still disagree on the effect wolves have on the size of prey populations. Wolves may kill livestock and dogs when they have the opportunity, yet many wolves that live near livestock rarely, if ever, kill them. The number of stock killed in North America is small but increasing as wolves expand their range. During the 1990s average annual losses to wolves in Minnesota were 72 cattle, 33 sheep, and 648 turkeys, plus a few individuals of other types of livestock. Stock losses are higher in Eurasia. In some areas wolves survive only by killing livestock and eating livestock carrion and human garbage. Nonetheless, wolves usually avoid contact with humans. There have been few substantiated wolf attacks on humans in North America. Such attacks are unusual but have occurred in Eurasia and India and sometimes have resulted in death.

Wolves have few natural enemies other than man. They can live up to 13 years in the wild, but most die long before that age. Diseases and parasites that can affect wolves include canine parvovirus, distemper, rabies, blastomycosis, Lyme disease, lice, mange, and heartworm. In most areas of the world, humans are the leading cause of death for wolves. In areas of high wolf density and declining prey populations, the major causes of death are killing by other wolves and starvation.

OTHER WOLVES

The red wolf (*C. rufus*) is tawny, reddish, or black. It grows to a length of about 105 to 125 cm (41 to 49 inches), excluding the tail, which is 33 to 43 cm (13 to 17 inches) long, and weighs about 20 to 37 kg (44 to 82 pounds). The red wolf is an endangered species that formerly roamed through the southeastern United States as far west as Texas. Following extinction in the wild, captive-reared red wolves were reintroduced to coastal North Carolina.

A small population of fewer than 100 has become established, but the species is threatened by hybridization with coyotes. Some experts believe the red wolf to be a subspecies of gray wolf or a hybrid between the gray wolf and the coyote.

The critically endangered Abyssinian wolf (*C. simensis*) also looks similar to the coyote. It lives in a few isolated areas of grassland and heath scrub at high elevations in Ethiopia. Although they live in packs, the wolves hunt alone for rodents and other small mammals. The Abyssinian wolf was once considered to be a type of jackal.

Genetic evidence suggests that the Falkland Islands, or Antarctic, wolf (*Dusicyon australis*), now extinct, diverged from North American wolves some six million years ago. Although the Isthmus of Panama, which allowed the migration of canids to South America, did not form until 2.5 million years ago, *D. australis* was somehow able to reach the Falklands.

The dire wolf (*C. dirus*) was common in western North America during the Pleistocene Epoch but is now extinct. It was the largest known wolf, being half again as large as the modern gray wolf.

BUSH DOGS

The bush dog (*Speothos venaticus*), also called the savannah dog, is a small, stocky carnivore of the family Canidae found in the forests and savannas of Central and South America. The bush dog is a rare species, and its numbers are declining as a result of the destruction of its natural habitat. The bush dog has short legs and long hair and grows to a shoulder height of about 30 cm (12 inches). It is 58 to 75 cm long, exclusive of its 13- to 15-cm tail. It weighs about 5 to 7 kg (11 to 15 pounds) and is brown with reddish or whitish forequarters and dark hindquarters and tail. Little is known of its habits, though it is reported to be nocturnal, to hunt in packs, and to feed largely on rodents.

COYOTES

The coyote (*Canis latrans*), also called the prairie wolf or brush wolf, is a New World member of the dog family (Canidae) that is smaller and more lightly built than the wolf. The coyote, whose name is derived from the Aztec *coyotl*, is found from Alaska southward into Central America, but especially on the Great Plains. Historically, the eastern border of its range was the Appalachians, but the coyote has expanded its range and now can be found throughout the United States and Canada.

The coyote stands about 60 cm (24 inches) at the shoulder, weighs about 9 to 23 kg (20 to 50 pounds), and is about 1 to 1.3 metres (3.3 to 4.3 feet) long, including its 30- to 40-cm (12- to 16-inch) tail. The fur is long and coarse and is generally grizzled buff above and whitish below, reddish on the legs, and bushy on the black-tipped

A lighter-coloured variant of the coyote (Canis latrans). © Corbis

tail. There is, however, considerable local variation in size and colour, with the largest animals living in the northeastern United States and eastern Canada.

Noted for its nightly serenades of yaps and howls, the coyote is primarily nocturnal, running with tail pointed downward and sometimes attaining a speed of 65 km (40 miles) per hour. Coyotes are extremely efficient hunters, and their senses are keen. They are visual predators in open areas, but they mostly use smell and hearing to locate prey in thick vegetation or forest. In the northern parts of its range, the coyote relies primarily on the snowshoe hare and white-tailed deer as prey. A single coyote is able to capture an adult deer, especially in deep snow. Coyotes take down deer by repeatedly biting at the back legs and hindquarters, the kill finally being made with a choking bite to the throat. In fall and early winter, coyotes often hunt in pairs or packs, and the success of a pack increases with its size. Larger packs typically hunt larger animals, although they will capture and eat whatever prey they encounter. The coyote also consumes carrion. Wherever or whenever prey is unavailable or hard to obtain, coyotes eat large quantities of wild berries and fruits. In doing so, they may become much leaner. In the northeast, coyotes are fatter during winter, when deer are easier to capture, than in late summer.

The coyote competes with several other carnivores, especially in the northeast, where coyotes were previously absent. Lynx and bobcats compete for the same foods (hares and rabbits), and the success of each of these predators depends on the setting. Lynx are better at catching hares in powdery snow, whereas coyotes hunt in areas with less snow accumulation where travel is easier. The coyote also competes with the red fox, which it will kill upon encountering. For this reason, areas with high coyote densities often harbour few red foxes. Occasionally, larger animals such as wolves or cougars prey on coyotes.

Coyotes mate between January and March, and females usually bear four to seven pups after a gestation of 58 to 65 days. Births occur in an underground burrow, usually a hole dug by badgers or by the parent coyotes. Most dens are on hillsides with good drainage (to avoid flooding during rainstorms) and where visibility allows parents to watch the surroundings for danger. Young are born blind and helpless, but, after two to three weeks, pups start emerging from the den to play. Weaning occurs at five to seven weeks, and both parents feed and care for the pups until they are fully grown and independent, usually at six to nine months of age. Young typically disperse in the fall, but some older siblings will help raise younger offspring, and family groups may remain together and form packs during winter.

Coyotes are territorial, and both members of a breeding pair defend the territory against other coyotes. Territories are marked with urine and feces, and it is believed that howling may serve to indicate occupancy of a territory. The size of coyote territories varies among habitats and also depends on its abundance of prey. Most territories, however, range from 10 to 40 square km (4 to 15 square miles).

Coyotes may live up to 21 years or more in captivity, but in the wild few animals live more than 6 to 8 years. Most deaths are now caused by humans, whether for the animals' fur, for management of domestic or game animals, or because of collisions with vehicles. In the wild, infectious diseases such as mange, canine distemper, and rabies probably are the most common causes of death.

TERRITORIAL BEHAVIOUR

Territorial behaviour is the group of methods by which an animal, or group of animals, protects its territory from incursions by others of its species. Territorial boundaries may be marked by sounds such as bird song, or scents such as pheromones secreted by the skin glands of many mammals. If such advertisement does not discourage intruders, chases and fighting follow.

Territorial behaviour is adaptive in many ways; it may permit an animal to mate without interruption or to raise its young in an area where there will be little competition for food. It can also prevent overcrowding by maintaining an optimum distance among members of a population. Territories may be seasonal; in many songbirds the mated pair defends the nest and feeding area until after the young are fledged. In communally nesting birds such as gulls, the territory may simply consist of the nest itself.

Wolf packs maintain territories in which they hunt and live. These areas are aggressively defended from all non-pack members. The male cougar has a large territory that may overlap the territories of several females but is defended against other males. Responding to scent marks, the inhabitants of the overlapping ranges also avoid each other, except for breeding.

Mange is easily detected, as infected coyotes begin to lose fur on parts of their bodies, usually starting at the tail and flanks. Eventually they may die of exposure when the weather turns cold.

An intelligent animal with a reputation for cunning and swiftness, the coyote has long been persecuted because of its predation on domestic or game animals. Until the middle of the 20th century, many states paid bounties for coyotes. Near farms coyotes commonly take livestock, especially sheep. They also can cause damage to fields of ripe watermelon, honeydew, and other market fruits. Near cities coyotes have been known to kill and eat pets left outside overnight. There are several reported cases of attacks on humans, including at least one fatality. However, such events are extremely rare and typically occur where coyotes have lost their fear of humans, such as near suburban areas. Coyotes generally fear and avoid humans, but they habituate well to human presence in parks and cities and are found with regularity in urban settings such as Chicago and Los Angeles.

Coyote populations at the start of the 21st century were greater than ever before in North America, a strong testament to this canine's ability to adapt and thrive in human-modified landscapes. Despite constant hunting, poisoning, and other means of control in some localities, the coyote persists, and its future seems secure. Indeed, management of coyotes by biologists is concerned more with their overabundance than their rarity. The coyote hybridizes readily with the domestic dog (*Canis lupus familiaris*); the offspring are called coydogs.

DINGOES

The dingo, also called the warrigal, is a feral canine native to Australia. Most authorities regard dingoes as either a subspecies of the domestic dog (*Canis lupus familiaris dingo*) or a subspecies of the wolf (*C. lupus dingo*); however, some authorities consider dingoes to be their own species (*C. dingo*). The name *dingo* is also used to describe wild dogs of Malaysia, Thailand, the Philippines, and New Guinea. The dingo was apparently introduced from Asia to other regions by sea travelers, probably 3,500 to 4,000 years ago. The oldest known dingo fossil in Australia dates from about 3,500 years ago. (By contrast, humans arrived in Australia at least 30,000 years ago.) It is believed by many authorities that dingoes were introduced to

Australia before true domestication of dogs was achieved, thus allowing establishment of wild populations. Dingoes are therefore regarded by these authorities not as feral descendants of once-domesticated dogs but rather as truly wild versions of the domestic dog.

Similar to the domestic dog in structure and habits, the dingo has short, soft fur, a bushy tail, and erect, pointed ears. It is about 120 cm (48 inches) long, including the 30-cm (12-inch) tail, stands about 60 cm (24 inches) tall at the shoulder, and weighs about 20 kg (44 pounds). Its colour varies between yellowish and reddish brown, often with white underparts, paws, and tail tip. Dingoes can be differentiated from domestic dogs of similar size and shape by their longer muzzle, larger ears, more-massive molars, and longer and more-slender canine teeth.

Dingo (Canis dingo, C. lupus familiaris dingo, *or* C. lupus dingo). G.R. Roberts

Dingoes hunt alone or in small groups of 2 to 12 individuals. Groups typically consist of family members
and resemble those of other canines such as wolves.
Dingoes are highly mobile; daily movements may reach
10 to 20 km (6 to 12 miles), and territories vary in size
from 10 to 115 square km (4 to 44 square miles). There
is little overlap among adjacent groups; boundaries are
delineated by scent marking, and occupancy of territories is also indicated by howling. Dingoes rarely bark,
but they have a varied repertoire of howls, often being
called "singing dogs."

Dingoes are large carnivores. Historically, they
preyed mostly on kangaroos and wallabies, but their
diet changed with the introduction of the European
rabbit (genus *Oryctolagus*) into Australia in the mid-
19th century. Now dingoes consume mostly rabbits and
small rodents. Through competition they may have contributed to the extermination of the native Tasmanian
wolf and Tasmanian devil (both marsupials) from the
Australian mainland.

DHOLES

The dhole (*Cuon alpinus*), also called the red dog, is a wild Asian
carnivore of the dog family (Canidae), found in central and southeastern wooded areas and distinguished structurally by the lack of
one pair of lower molars. Its length ranges between 76 and 100 cm
(30 and 40 inches), exclusive of the 28- to 48-cm (11- to 19-inch) tail,
and its weight is from 14 to 21 kg (30 to 46 pounds). Coloration varies from yellowish to reddish brown, often with lighter underparts.
Dholes hunt various mammals, generally associating in packs of up
to 30 individuals; they usually hunt such prey as deer and wild sheep
but are reported to attack animals as large as tigers and bears. A
litter usually contains two to six pups, born after a nine-week gestation period.

Occasionally, dingoes prey on livestock, especially calves, and for this reason they are often regarded as pests. With the European settlement of Australia, they preyed on sheep and poultry and were consequently eliminated from most areas. Today the purity of dingo populations is under threat from hybridization with domestic dogs, a problem that is constantly increasing with spreading human settlement. Wild dingoes, though bold and suspicious, can be tamed, and they are sometimes captured and tamed by Aborigines.

Dingoes have their pups in caves, hollow logs, and enlarged rabbit warrens. Breeding occurs in the spring, and, after a gestation period of 63 days, females give birth to four to five pups (occasionally up to 10). As with most other canines, both parents care for the young. Young males often disperse outside their natal areas; one tagged individual was recorded as traveling 250 km (150 miles) in 10 months. The longest known life span for any individual dingo is 14 years 9 months.

Raccoon Dogs

The raccoon dog (*Nyctereutes procyonoides*) is a member of the dog family (Canidae) native to eastern Asia and introduced into Europe. Some authorities place it in the raccoon family, Procyonidae. It resembles the raccoon in having dark facial markings that contrast with its yellowish brown coat, but it does not have a ringed tail. It has short, brown or blackish limbs, a heavy body, and rounded ears. Head and body length is 50 to 65 cm (20 to 26 inches); tail length, 13 to 18 cm (5 to 8 inches); and weight, about 7.5 kg (16.5 pounds). Most active at night, the raccoon dog is omnivorous and feeds on small animals, fish, vegetation, and carrion. Litters contain 5 to 12 young, born after a

Raccoon dogs (Nyctereutes procyonoides). Russ Kinne/Photo Researchers

gestation period reported at 60 to 79 days. The long fur of the raccoon dog is sold commercially as "Ussuri raccoon," or "tanuki."

JACKALS

A jackal is any of several species of wolflike carnivores of the dog genus *Canis,* family Canidae, sharing with the hyena an exaggerated reputation for cowardice. Three species are usually recognized: the golden, or Asiatic, jackal (*C. aureus*), found from eastern Europe and northeast Africa to Southeast Asia, and the black-backed jackal (*C. mesomelas*) and side-striped jackal (*C. adustus*) of southern and eastern

Black-backed jackal (Canis mesomelas). Leonard Lee Rue III

Africa. Jackals grow to a length of about 85 to 95 cm (34 to 37 inches), including the 30- to 35-cm (12- to 14-inch) tail, and weigh about 7 to 11 kg (15 to 24 pounds). The golden jackal is yellowish, the black-backed jackal is rusty red with a black back, and the side-striped jackal is grayish with a white-tipped tail and an indistinct stripe on each side.

Jackals inhabit open country. They are nocturnal animals that usually conceal themselves by day in brush or thickets and sally forth at dusk to hunt. They live alone, in pairs, or in packs and feed on whatever small animals, plant material, or carrion is available. They follow lions and other large cats in order to finish a carcass when the larger animal has eaten its fill. When hunting in packs, they are able to bring down prey as large as an antelope or sheep.

Like other members of the genus, jackals sing at evening; their cry is considered more dismaying to human ears than that of the hyena. They have an offensive odour caused by the secretion of a gland at the base of the tail.

AFRICAN HUNTING DOGS

The African hunting dog (*Lycaon pictus*), also called the Cape hunting dog or hyena dog, is a wild African carnivore that differs from the rest of the members of the dog family (Canidae) in having only four toes on each foot. Its coat is short, sparse, and irregularly blotched with yellow, black, and white. The African hunting dog is about 76 to 102 cm (30 to 41 inches) long, exclusive of its 30- to 40-cm (12- to 16-inch) tail, stands about 60 cm (24 inches) at the shoulder, and weighs about 16 to 23 kg (35 to 50 pounds).

The African hunting dog is long-limbed with a broad, flat head, short muzzle, and large, erect ears. It hunts in packs of 15 to 60 or more and is found in most of Africa south and east of the Sahara, particularly in grasslands. It usually preys on antelopes and some larger game but has been hunted in settled regions for the damage it sometimes does to domestic livestock. The average number of young per litter appears to be about six; gestation periods of about 60 and 80 days have been noted.

The young are born in burrows, the litters containing two to seven pups; gestation lasts 57 to 70 days. Like wolves and coyotes, jackals interbreed with domestic dogs.

The aardwolf, family Hyaenidae, is sometimes called a maned, or gray, jackal. The South American fox, *Dusicyon*, is sometimes referred to as a jackal.

FOXLIKE CANINES

Foxes are various members of the family Canidae resembling small to medium-sized bushy-tailed dogs with long fur, pointed ears, and narrow snouts. In a restricted sense, the name refers to the 10 or so species classified as "true" foxes (genus *Vulpes*), especially the red, or common, fox (*V. vulpes*), which lives in both the Old World and the New World. However, several other animals referred to as foxes belong to genera other than *Vulpes*, including the North American gray fox, five species of South American fox, the Arctic fox (includes the blue fox), the bat-eared fox, and the crab-eating fox.

RED FOXES

Widely held as a symbol of animal cunning, the red fox (*Vulpes vulpes*) is the subject of considerable folklore. The red fox has the largest natural distribution of any land mammal except human beings. In the Old World it ranges over virtually all of Europe, temperate Asia, and northern Africa; in the New World it inhabits most of North America. Introduced to Australia, it has established itself throughout much of the continent. The red fox has a coat of long guard hairs, soft, fine underfur that is typically a rich reddish brown, often a white-tipped tail, and black ears and legs. Colour, however, is variable; in North America black and silver coats are found, with a variable amount of white or white-banded hair occurring in a black coat. A form called the cross fox (or brant fox) is yellowish brown with a black cross extending between the shoulders and down the back; it is found in both North America and the Old World. The Samson fox is a mutant strain of red fox found in northwestern Europe. It lacks the long guard hairs, and the underfur is tightly curled.

Red foxes are generally about 90 to 105 cm (36 to 42 inches) long (about 35 to 40 cm of this being tail), stand about 40 cm at the shoulder, and weigh about 5 to 7 kg (10 to 15 pounds). Their preferred habitats are mixed landscapes, but they live in environments ranging from Arctic tundra to arid desert. Red foxes adapt very well to human presence, thriving in areas with farmland and woods, and populations can be found in many large cities and suburbs. Mice, voles, and rabbits, as well as eggs, fruit, and birds, make up most of the diet, but foxes readily eat other available food such as carrion, grain (especially sunflower seeds), garbage, pet food left unattended overnight, and domestic poultry. On the prairies of North America, it is estimated that red foxes kill close to a million wild ducks each year. Their impact on domestic birds and some wild game birds has led to their numbers often being regulated near game farms and bird-production areas.

MOST CRAFTY OF ALL BEASTS

"The fox is a great nuisance to the husbandman," declares the writer of the article "Fox" in the first edition of *Encyclopædia Britannica* (1768). The reader is then directed to the article "Canis," where the wily raider of chicken coops is described further:

> *He is esteemed to be the most crafty of all beasts of prey. His craftiness is chiefly discovered by the schemes he falls upon in order to catch lambs, geese, hens, and all kinds of small birds....When the fox has acquired a larger prey than it can devour at once, it never begins to feed till it has secured the rest, which it does with great address. It digs holes in different places; returns to the spot where it had left the booty; and (supposing a whole flock of poultry to have been its prey) will bring*

Fox, engraving by Andrew Bell, from Encyclopædia Britannica, first edition (1768). Encyclopædia Britannica, Inc.

them one by one, and thrust them in with its nose, and then conceal them till the calls of hunger incite him to pay them another visit. Of all animals the fox has the most significant eye, by which it expresses every passion of love, fear, hatred, etc. It is remarkably playful; but, like all savage creatures half reclaimed, will on the least offence bite those it is most familiar with. It is a great admirer of its bushy tail, with which it frequently amuses and exercises itself, by running in circles to catch it: and, in cold weather, wraps it round its nose.

Readers ambitious to trap and destroy this "beast of chace" are directed to the article "Hunting," but not without dire forewarning:

The smell of this animal is in general very strong, but that of the urine is remarkably fetid....The smell is so offensive, that it has often proved the means of the foxes escape from the dogs; who have so strong an aversion at the filthy effluvia, as to avoid encountering the animal it came from.

The red fox is hunted for sport and for its pelt, which is a mainstay of the fur trade. Fox pelts, especially those of silver foxes, are commonly produced on fox farms, where the animals are raised until they are fully grown at approximately 10 months of age. In much of their range, red foxes are the primary carrier of rabies. Several countries, especially the United Kingdom and France, have extensive culling and vaccination programs aimed at reducing the incidence of rabies in red foxes.

Red foxes mate in winter. After a gestation period of seven or eight weeks, the female (vixen) gives birth to 1 to 10 or more (5 is average) young, called cubs or pups. Birth takes place in a den, which is commonly a burrow abandoned by another animal. It is often enlarged by the parent foxes. The cubs remain in the den for about five weeks and are cared for by both parents throughout the summer. The young disperse in the fall once they are fully grown and independent.

"White" phase of Arctic fox changing to its summer coat. Russ Kinne—
Photo Researchers/EB Inc.

ARCTIC FOXES

The Arctic fox (*Alopex lagopus*), also called the white fox
or polar fox, is a member of the family Canidae, found
throughout the Arctic, usually on tundra or mountains
near the sea. In adaptation to the climate, it has short,
rounded ears, a short muzzle, and fur-covered soles. Its
length is about 50 to 60 cm (20 to 24 inches), exclusive of
the 30-cm (12-inch) tail; and its weight is about 3 to 8 kg (6.6
to 17 pounds). Coloration depends on whether the animal
is of the "white" or the "blue" colour phase. Individuals of
the white phase are grayish brown in summer and white in
winter, while those of the blue phase (blue foxes of the fur
trade) are grayish in summer and gray-blue in winter.

The Arctic fox is a burrow dweller and may be active
at any time of day. It feeds on whatever animal or vegetable material is available and often follows polar bears

BAT-EARED FOXES

Bat-eared fox (Otocyon megalotis). Mark Boulton—The National Audubon Society Collection/Photo Researchers

The bat-eared fox (*Otocyon megalotis*), also called the Cape fox, big-eared fox, or motlosi, is a large-eared member of the dog family (Canidae), found in open, arid areas of eastern and southern Africa. It has 48 teeth, 6 more than any other canid. The bat-eared fox is like the red fox in appearance but has unusually large ears. It is yellowish gray with black face and legs and black-tipped ears and tail. It grows to a length of about 80 cm (32 inches), including a 30-cm (12-inch) tail, and weighs from 3 to 4.5 kg (6.6 to 10 pounds). It lives alone or in small groups and feeds primarily on insects, especially termites. Litters contain two to five young; gestation lasts 60 to 70 days.

to feed on the remains of their kills. It usually breeds once yearly, a litter of up to 14 dark-furred pups being born between April and June; gestation is about 52 days.

CRAB-EATING FOXES

The crab-eating fox (*Cerdocyon thous*), also called the savanna fox or crab-eating dog, is a South American member of the dog family (Canidae), found in grassy or forested areas. It attains a length of 60 to 70 cm (24 to 28 inches), excluding a 30-cm (12-inch) tail, and has a gray to brown coat that is frequently tinged with yellow. It generally lives alone or in pairs and spends the day in a burrow, emerging at night to hunt for such foods as small animals, fruit, insects, turtle eggs, fowl, and of course, crabs. It is easily tamed and is sometimes kept as a pet by Indians.

FENNECS

The fennec (*Fennecus zerda*) is a desert-dwelling member of the dog family (Canidae), found in north Africa and the Sinai and Arabian peninsulas. The fennec is characterized by its small size (head and body length 36 to 41 cm [14 to 16 inches], weight about 1.5 kg [3.3 pounds]) and large ears (15 cm [6 inches] or more in length). It has long, thick, whitish to sand-coloured fur and a black-tipped tail 18 to 30 cm (7 to 12 inches) long. Mainly nocturnal, the fennec spends the heat of the day underground in its burrow. It feeds on insects, small animals, and fruit. Its litters of two to five young are born after a gestation period of about 51 days.

The name *fennec* is sometimes erroneously applied to the South African silver fox (*Vulpes chama*) and to Ruppell's fox (*V. ruppelli*).

GRAY FOXES

The gray fox (*Urocyon cinereoargenteus*) is a grizzled, gray-furred New World fox of the family Canidae. It is found in forested, rocky, and brush-covered country from Canada to northern South America. Distinguished by the reddish colour on its neck, ears, and legs, the gray fox grows to a length of about 50 to 75 cm (20 to 30 inches), excluding its 30- to 40-cm (12- to 16-inch) tail, and a weight of about 3 to 6 kg (7 to 13 pounds). It is more retiring and less crafty than the red fox, and unlike other foxes it commonly climbs trees. The gray fox is primarily nocturnal and takes a variety of foods, including small birds and mammals, insects, and fruit. Its two to seven dark-furred pups are born in spring, after a gestation of about 63 days.

MANED WOLVES

A maned wolf (*Chrysocyon brachyurus*) is a rare, large-eared member of the dog family (Canidae) found in remote plains areas of central South America. The maned wolf has a foxlike head, long reddish brown fur, very long blackish legs, and an erectile mane. Its length ranges from 125 to 130 cm (50 to 52 inches), excluding the 30- to 40-cm (12- to 16-inch) tail. Its shoulder height is about 75 cm (30 inches), and its weight is approximately 23 kg (50 pounds). A solitary animal, the maned wolf is primarily nocturnal and feeds on small animals, insects, and plant material. It attacks sheep but generally avoids human contact.

The gray fox, though it may sometimes raid hen houses, is beneficial in controlling the rodent population; its fur is often sold but is not of great value. A closely related but smaller form, the island gray fox (*U. littoralis*), is found on islands off the coast of southern California.

SOUTH AMERICAN FOXES

The South American fox (*Pseudalopex*), also called the South American dog or South American jackal, is any of five members of the dog family (Canidae) that resemble true foxes, though they are not species of the true fox genus, *Vulpes*.

In general, South American foxes are long-haired, rather grayish animals that grow to about 0.5 to 1 metre (1.6 to 3.3 feet) in length, excluding the bushy tail, which is 25 to 50 cm (10 to 20 inches) long. They are found in open terrain as opposed to thick forest, and they feed on small animals, birds, fruit and other plant material, and insects. Generally nocturnal, they live in abandoned burrows or in dens among rocks or trees. Both parents care for the litters of one to eight young. South American foxes can attack domestic livestock, but they are helpful in controlling rodent populations.

CHAPTER 4
FELINES

A feline, or felid, is any of 37 species of swift, agile, sharp-clawed carnivorous mammals that belong to the cat family, Felidae. Among others, felines include the cheetah, puma, jaguar, leopard, lion, lynx, tiger, and domestic cat. Cats are native to almost every region on Earth, with the exception of Australia and Antarctica. They live in a wide variety of habitats, but they are typically woodland animals.

Most cats are patterned with spots, stripes, or rosettes, but some, such as the puma (*Puma concolor*), jaguarundi (*Herpailurus yaguarondi*), and lion (*Panthera leo*), are uniform in colour. Black or nearly black coats occur in individuals of several species. Although lynx (genus *Lynx*) have a stubby tail, most cats have a long tail that makes up about a third of the animal's total length. The head is characterized by a short nose and round face, usually with short ears. The only cat with a well-developed mane is the male African lion. Cat feet have sharp claws that are retractile except in the cheetah. In most felids the male is larger than the female.

Cats are noted for purring when content and for snarling, howling, or spitting when in conflict with another of their kind. The so-called "big cats" (genus *Panthera*), especially the lion, often roar, growl, or shriek. Usually, however, cats are silent. Many cats use "clawing trees," upon which they leave the marks of their claws as they stand and drag their front feet downward with the claws extended. Whether such behaviour is for the purpose of cleaning or sharpening the claws or simply to stretch is debatable, but the behaviour is innate; kittens raised in isolation soon begin to claw objects.

Ocelot (Leopardus pardalis). Warren Garst/Tom Stack and Associates

The larger cats are strong, fierce, and extremely dangerous when hungry. Because of their large size, they occasionally attack humans. Although tigers and leopards are most noted as man-eaters, lions and jaguars can also be dangerous. In North America the puma, also known as the cougar or mountain lion, tends to avoid contact with humans, but a few attacks occur annually, especially in areas where development encroaches on areas of high puma density, such as the western United States. Similarly, attacks on livestock often necessitate removal of problem animals.

The fur of some cats is sometimes in great demand, especially fur with contrasting colours and patterns such as spots or stripes. The demand is such that some rare cats are hunted and trapped illegally and are in danger of becoming extinct. In North America none of the cats used by the fur

Canada lynx (Lynx canadensis). Philip Wayre/EB Inc.

trade is endangered. Strict regulations allow a sustainable take of animals from healthy populations of Canada lynx (*Lynx canadensis*), bobcat (*Lynx rufus*), and puma.

NATURAL HISTORY

The lion, tiger (*Panthera tigris*), and cheetah (*Acinonyx jubatus*) are mainly terrestrial, but they are agile climbers; the leopard (*Panthera pardus*), jaguar (*P. onca*), ocelot (*Leopardus pardalis*), and other cats are very much at home in trees. The larger cats range over large areas, often roving alone or with a companion. Occasionally one may become a member of a family group. Only lions are gregarious, with prides consisting of as many as 30 individuals.

Almost all cats feed on small mammals and birds or on large herbivores such as deer and various types of antelope. The fishing cat (*Prionailurus viverrinus*) feeds largely on fishes and clams or snails and thus fits into a slightly different niche than that of most cats. The flat-headed cat (*Prionailurus planiceps*) is the only species known to feed to any extent on vegetation such as fruit and sweet potatoes. Food caching occurs in larger cats, and some may drag their kill into a tree or place it under a bush after the initial gorging. Cats live on a feast-or-famine routine, gorging themselves when a kill is made and then fasting for several days.

Most hunting is done using vision and hearing. Typically solitary while hunting, a cat steals up to its prey on padded feet. Long, sensitive whiskers on the face aid the cat during the stalking of the prey by brushing against obstacles and enabling the cat to avoid making excessive noise. When close to its prey, the cat overwhelms it in a short, quick rush or leap. Cats can move very fast in a short dash but are not built for sustained speed. The cheetah, which usually hunts during the day, is credited with being

Clouded leopard (Neofelis nebulosa). © Digital Vision/Getty Images

the speediest of mammals, capable of speeds of more than 100 km per hour (62 mph). Cats rely on superior speed and reflexes to overtake their dodging prey, which often has greater endurance. If overtaken, the prey is thrown down and dispatched with a deep bite, usually to the neck.

The gestation period of most smaller cats is approximately two months, and that of the larger cats is closer to four months. One to six kittens make up the usual litter. Female cats may have from four to eight nipples. The breeding season usually is in the late winter or early spring. Some cats (lions, tigers, and leopards) are capable of breeding at any time during the year, and many species are induced ovulators, ovulation being induced by hormones released during copulation. The size of the animal does not seem to determine the litter size, number of litters, or time of the breeding season. In the larger cats, however, the initial breeding age is older; the females may be three or four years of age and males as old as five or six. Smaller cats may breed when less than a year old. Most litters are born in places seldom disturbed, such as in a rocky cavern, under a fallen tree, or in a dense thicket. The serval (*Leptailurus serval*) uses an old porcupine or aardvark burrow. In most species the male does not aid in the care and raising of the young, and in fact the female may have to guard against his attacks on the kittens.

FORM AND FUNCTION

The agility of a cat is evident in its anatomy. The clavicle, or collarbone, is much reduced in size. It does not connect with other bones but is buried in the muscles of the shoulder region. This allows the animal to spring on its prey without danger of breaking the bone. The hind legs are well developed, with powerful muscles that propel the cat in its spring toward or onto prey. In addition to the power of the hind legs, the animal uses strong back muscles to straighten the spinal column and provide extra force in springing and running.

Cats are generally nocturnal in habit. Their large eyes are especially adapted for seeing at night. The retina has a layer of guanine called the tapetum lucidum, which reflects light and causes the eyes to shine at night when illuminated. Cats have good senses of sight and hearing, but their sense of smell is not as developed as that of the canids, a fact suggested by the cat's short snout.

A predisposition to cleanliness is well established among cats. They groom themselves with their rasping tongue, preening at length after a meal. Feces and urine are covered as a matter of habit. Cats differ in their reaction to water; most species are reluctant to enter it but will swim readily when necessary. Nervous tail wagging is common to all cats, from the lion to the house cat. Kittens learn it from the mother; the behaviour is associated with play, which is a prelude to predation as an adult.

Cats are the most highly specialized of the terrestrial flesh-eating mammals. They are powerfully built, with a large brain and strong teeth. The teeth are adapted to three functions: stabbing (canines), anchoring (canines), and cutting (carnassial molars). Cats have no flat-crowned crushing teeth and thus do not chew or grind their food but instead cut it. All cats are adapted to be strict flesh eaters, an assumption made primarily on the basis of their digestive tract and dentition. In keeping with a carnivorous habit, the cat has a simple gut; the small intestine is only about three times the length of the body. The tongue in all cats has a patch of sharp, backward-directed spines near the tip, which has the appearance and feel of a coarse file; these spines help the cat lap up liquids and groom itself. There are five padded toes on the front foot

Burmese, sable. © Paddy Cutts/Animals Unlimited

and four on the rear. The first toe and its pad on the front foot are raised so that only four toes register in a track.

Cats have a reduced number of premolar and molar teeth; the typical dental formula includes only 30 teeth. The incisors are small and chisel-like, the canines long and pointed. The premolars are sharp, and occasionally an upper premolar may be lacking. The lower molar is elongate and sharp, the upper molar rudimentary. Because of the reduction in the number and size of the cheek teeth, a space remains between the canines and premolars in all cats except the cheetah. Felids form the most strictly carnivorous group in the order Carnivora, and the highly developed carnassial teeth reflect this specialized food habit. There is little if any specialization in the teeth for grinding or chewing. The strong masseter muscles, which raise the lower jaw, restrict lateral movement. The jaw primarily moves vertically for holding the prey in a viselike grip and for slicing off pieces of meat with the carnassials. Meat is thus cut off and swallowed in relatively unchewed chunks that are broken down by strong enzymes and acids in the digestive tract.

EVOLUTION

The history of the cat family can be traced through the fossil record to the Late Eocene Epoch (about 37 million years ago). The "cat pattern" seems to have been established very early in the evolution of mammals, for the early cats were already typical cats at a time when the ancestors of most other modern mammalian species were scarcely recognizable. Cats of the subfamily Felinae, which includes the domestic cat (*Felis catus*), appeared about 10 million years ago and have continued almost unchanged into modern times.

LARGER WILD FELINES

The best known "big cats" belong to genus *Panthera*; they are the lions, tigers, jaguars, and leopards. Some species of other genera, however, are well known for their power, speed, and hunting prowess; among these are the cheetah and the puma, or mountain lion.

LIONS

The lion (*Panthera leo*) is a large, powerfully built cat that is second in size only to the tiger. The proverbial "king of beasts," the lion has been one of the best-known wild animals since earliest times. Lions are most active at night and live in a variety of habitats but prefer grassland, savanna, dense scrub, and open woodland. Historically, they ranged across much of Europe, Asia, and Africa, but now they are found mainly in parts of Africa south of the Sahara. About 200 Asiatic lions constitute a slightly smaller race that lives under strict protection in India's Gir National Park and Wildlife Sanctuary.

The lion is a well-muscled cat with a long body, large head, and short legs. Size and appearance vary considerably between the sexes. The male's outstanding characteristic is his mane, which varies between different individuals and populations. It may be entirely lacking; it may fringe the face; or it may be full and shaggy, covering the back of the head, neck, and shoulders and continuing onto the throat and chest to join a fringe along the belly. In some lions the mane and fringe are very dark, almost black, giving the cat a majestic appearance. Manes make males look larger and may serve to intimidate rivals or impress prospective mates. A full-grown male is about 1.8 to 2.1 metres (6 to 7 feet) long, excluding the 1-metre (40-inch) tail; he

Lioness (Panthera leo) *with cubs.* Erwin and Peggy Bauer/Bruce Coleman Ltd.

stands about 1.2 metres (4 feet) high at the shoulder and weighs 170 to 230 kg (370 to 500 pounds). The female, or lioness, is smaller, with a body length of 1.5 metres (5 feet), a shoulder height of 0.9 to 1.1 metres (3 to 3.6 feet), and a weight of 120 to 180 kg (265 to 400 pounds). The lion's coat is short and varies in colour from buff yellow, orange-brown, or silvery gray to dark brown, with a tuft on the tail tip that is usually darker than the rest of the coat.

Lions are unique among cats in that they live in a group, or pride. The members of a pride typically spend the day in several scattered groups that may unite to hunt or share a meal. A pride consists of several generations of lionesses, some of which are related, a smaller number of breeding males, and their cubs. The group may consist of as few as 4 or as many as 37 members, but about 15 is the average size. Each pride has a well-defined territory consisting of a core area that is strictly defended against intruding lions and a fringe area where some overlap is tolerated. Where prey is abundant, a territory area may be as small as 20 square km (8 square miles), but if game is sparse, it may cover up to 400 square km (150 square miles). Some prides have been known to use the same territory for decades, passing the area on between females. Lions proclaim their territory by roaring and by scent marking. Their distinctive roar is generally delivered in the evening before a night's hunting and again before getting up at dawn. Males also proclaim their presence by urinating on bushes, trees, or simply on the ground, leaving a pungent scent behind. Defecation and rubbing against bushes leave different scent markings.

There are a number of competing evolutionary explanations for why lions form groups. Large body size and high density of their main prey probably make group life more efficient for females in terms of energy expenditure. Groups of females, for example, hunt more effectively and are better able to defend cubs against infanticidal males and their hunting territory against other females. The relative importance of these factors is debated, and it is not clear which was responsible for the establishment of group life and which are secondary benefits.

Lions prey on a large variety of animals ranging in size from rodents and baboons to water buffalo and hippopotamuses, but they predominantly hunt medium- to large-sized hoofed animals such as wildebeests, zebras, and antelopes. Prey preferences vary geographically as well as between neighbouring prides. Lions are known to take elephants and giraffes, but only if the individual is young or especially sick. They readily eat any meat they can find, including carrion and fresh kills that they scavenge or forcefully steal from hyenas, cheetahs, or wild dogs. Lionesses living in open savanna do most of the hunting, whereas males typically appropriate their meals from the female's kills. However, male lions are also adept hunters, and in some areas they hunt frequently. Pride males in scrub or wooded habitat spend less time with the females and hunt most of their own meals. Nomadic males must always secure their own food.

Though a group of hunting lions is potentially nature's most formidable predatory force on land, a high proportion of their hunts fail. The cats pay no attention to the wind's direction (which can carry their scent to their prey), and they tire after running short distances. Typically, they stalk prey from nearby cover and then burst forth to run it down in a short, rapid rush. After leaping on the prey, the lion lunges at its neck and bites until the animal has been strangled. Other members of the pride quickly crowd around to feed on the kill, usually fighting for access. Hunts are sometimes conducted in groups, with members of a pride encircling a herd or approaching it from opposite directions, then closing in for a kill in the resulting panic. The cats typically gorge themselves and then rest for several days in its vicinity. An adult male can consume more than 34 kg (75 pounds) of meat at a single meal and rest for a week before resuming the hunt. If prey is abundant, both sexes typically spend 21 to 22 hours a day resting, sleeping, or sitting and hunt for only 2 or 3 hours a day.

Both sexes are polygamous and breed throughout the year, but females are usually restricted to the one or two adult males of their pride. In captivity lions often breed every year, but in the wild they usually breed no more than once in two years. Females are receptive to mating for three or four days within a widely variable reproductive cycle. During this time a pair generally mates every 20 to 30 minutes, with up to 50 copulations per 24 hours. Such extended copulation not only stimulates ovulation in the female but also secures paternity for the male by excluding other males. The gestation period is about 108 days, and the litter size varies from one to six cubs, two to four being usual.

Newborn cubs are helpless and blind and have a thick coat with dark spots that usually disappear with maturity. Cubs are able to follow their mothers at about three months of age and are weaned by six or seven months. They begin participating in kills by 11 months but probably cannot survive on their own until they are two years old. Although lionesses will nurse cubs other than their own, they are surprisingly inattentive mothers and often leave their cubs alone for up to 24 hours. There is a corresponding high mortality rate (e.g., 86 percent in the Serengeti), but survival rates improve after the age of two. In the wild, sexual maturity is reached at three or four years of age. Some female cubs remain within the pride when they attain sexual maturity, but others are forced out and join other prides or wander as nomads. Male cubs are expelled from the pride at about three years of age and become nomads until they are old enough to try to take over another pride (after age five). Many adult males remain nomads for life. Mating opportunities for nomad males are rare, and competition between male lions to defend a pride's territory and mate with the pride females is fierce. Cooperating partnerships of two to four males are more successful at maintaining tenure with a pride than individuals, and larger coalitions father more surviving offspring per male. Small coalitions typically comprise related males, whereas larger groups often include unrelated individuals. If a new cohort of males is able to take over a pride, they will seek to kill young cubs sired by their predecessors. This has the effect of shortening the time before the cubs' mothers are ready to mate again. Females attempt to prevent this infanticide by hiding or directly defending their cubs; lionesses are generally more successful at protecting older cubs, as they would be leaving the pride sooner. In the wild lions seldom live more than 8 to 10 years, chiefly because of attacks by humans or other lions or the effects of kicks and gorings from intended prey animals. In captivity they may live 25 years or more.

During the Pleistocene Epoch (2,600,000 to 11,700 years ago), lions ranged across all of North America and Africa, through most of the Balkans, and across Anatolia and the Middle East into India. They disappeared from North America about 10,000 years ago, from the Balkans about 2,000 years ago, and from Palestine during the Crusades. By the 21st century their numbers had dwindled to a few tens of thousands, and those outside national parks are rapidly losing their habitat to agriculture. Conflict with humans, especially herders, outside parks is a major problem, and humans living around parks remain the predominant source of mortality for most populations. In 1994, for example, a variant of canine distemper caused the death of an estimated 1,000 lions at the Serengeti National Park. The apparent source of the virus was domestic dogs living along the periphery of the park. Despite such challenges, lion populations are healthy in many African reserves and at Gir, and they are a major tourist draw. High population densities of lions, however, can be a problem, not only for local ranchers but also for the cheetah and African wild dog—critically endangered carnivores that lose their kills, their cubs, and their lives to lions.

The genus *Panthera* includes leopards, jaguars, and tigers as well as lions. In captivity, lions have been induced to mate with other big cats. The offspring of a lion and a tigress is called a liger; that of a tiger and a lioness, a tigon; that of a leopard and a lioness, a leopon.

TIGERS

The tiger (*Panthera tigris*) is the largest member of the cat family (Felidae), rivaled only by the lion (*P. leo*) in strength and ferocity. Ranging from the Russian Far East through parts of North Korea, China, India, and Southeast Asia to the Indonesian island of Sumatra, all five remaining subspecies are endangered. The Siberian, or Amur, tiger (*P. tigris altaica*) is the largest, measuring up to 4 metres (13 feet) in total length and weighing up to 300 kg (660 pounds). The Indian, or Bengal, tiger (*P. tigris tigris*) is the most numerous and accounts for about half of the total tiger population. Males are larger than females and may attain a shoulder height of about 1 metre (40 inches) and a length of about 2.2 metres (7.25 feet), excluding a tail of about 1 metre; weight is 160 to 230 kg (350 to 500 pounds), and tigers from the south are smaller than those of the north.

The Bengal, Indo-Chinese (*P. tigris corbetti*), and Sumatran (*P. tigris sumatrae*) tigers are bright reddish tan, beautifully marked with dark, almost black, vertical stripes. The underparts, the inner sides of the limbs, the cheeks, and a large spot over each eye are whitish. The rare Siberian tiger has longer, softer, and paler fur. White tigers, not all of them true albinos, have occurred from time to time, almost all of them in India. Black tigers have been reported less frequently from the dense forests of Myanmar (Burma), Bangladesh, and eastern India. The tiger has no mane, but in old males the hair on the cheeks is rather long and spreading.

NATURAL HISTORY

The tiger has adapted to a great variety of environments, from the Siberian taiga, where nights can be as cold as -40 °C (-40 °F), to the mangrove swamps of the Sundarbans, where the temperatures reach more than 40 °C (104 °F).

Tigers haunt the ruins of buildings such as courts and temples and are at home in habitats ranging from dry grassland to rainforest. Grasslands, mixed grassland-forests, and deciduous rather than densely canopied forests support maximum population densities, as these habitats maintain the highest number of prey species. Having evolved in the temperate and subtropical forests of eastern Asia, the tiger is less tolerant of heat than other large cats, which may explain why it is an adept swimmer that appears to enjoy bathing. Under stress it may climb trees.

The tiger usually hunts by night and preys on a variety of animals, but it prefers fairly large prey such as deer (sambar, chital, and swamp deer) and wild pigs. A special liking for porcupines, despite the danger of injury from their quills, is an exception. Healthy large mammals are generally avoided, although there have been recorded instances of the tiger's having attacked elephants and adult water buffalo. Cattle are occasionally taken from human habitations, and some tigers can thrive on domestic livestock. After making a kill and consuming what it can, it makes a deliberate attempt to hide the carcass from vultures and other scavengers so that another meal can be obtained. Tigers are not averse to commandeering a kill from other tigers or leopards, and they sometimes eat carrion. Skill in killing and obtaining prey is only partly instinctive, maternal training being essential for proficiency. For this reason, tigers raised in captivity would not fare well if released into the wild. As the top predator throughout its range, the tiger plays a major role in controlling not only its prey population but that of other predators such as the leopard, dhole (Asiatic wild dog), and clouded leopard. No trait of the tiger has fascinated humans more than man eating. A number of reasons account for this—disability caused by age or injury, paucity of prey, acquisition of the habit from the mother, or defense of cubs or kill. With the reduction in the number of tigers, the occurrence of man-eating tigers has become rare except in the Sundarbans, the northeast Indian state of Uttar Pradesh, and neighbouring Nepal in and around Royal Chitwan National Park.

As solitary animals, tigers (especially males) establish and maintain their own territories, the size and nature of which vary with the number and distribution of prey, the presence of other tigers in the area, the nature of the terrain, the availability of water, and individual characteristics. Spacing between individuals and maintenance of territories are achieved through vocalization, scrapings on the ground, claw marking of trees, fecal deposits, scent deposited by the rubbing of facial glands, and spraying of urine mixed with scent secreted from the anal glands. The solitary nature of the species also helps minimize territorial conflict. Nonetheless, confrontations do occur, sometimes resulting in injury and even death.

The readiness of a tigress to mate is announced through vocalization and scent production. There is no fixed breeding season, though the preponderance of mating appears to occur in winter, with striped cubs being born after a gestation period of more than three months. The normal litter size is two to four, though up to seven cubs have been recorded. They are born blind, and, even when their eyes open, opacity prevents clear vision for six to eight weeks. There is thus a long period of weaning, tutelage, and training during which cub mortality is high, especially if food is scarce. During this time the offspring must endure long periods of absence by the mother while she is away hunting. Weaker cubs get less food because of the aggressiveness of their stronger siblings as food is less frequently made available. The cubs remain with the mother until about the second year, when they are nearly adult and are able to kill prey for themselves. Male cubs grow more quickly than females and tend to leave their mother earlier. Though cub infanticide (mainly by males) is known, it is not very unusual to find a male with a tigress and cubs, even sharing a kill. Such associations, however, do not last long. The tigress does not breed again until her cubs are independent. The average life span of a tiger in the wild is about 11 years.

TIGERS AND HUMANS

Next to the elephant and the lion, no wild animal is so frequently portrayed in Asian art and lore. The persistent practices of using tiger parts as talismans, tonics, or medicine, despite all scientific evidence contrary to their efficacy, are manifestations of beliefs that emanate from the aura of the tiger and the awe that it has inspired for millennia. Certain animist communities still worship the tiger. Every 12th year of the Chinese calendar is the year of

Siberian tiger (Panthera tigris altaica). Shutterstock.com

96

the tiger, and children born in it are considered especially lucky and powerful. In Hindu mythology the tiger is the *vahana* ("vehicle") of the goddess Durga. Tigers are represented on seals from the ancient Indus civilization. The greatest of the Gupta emperors of ancient India, Samudra, minted special gold coins depicting him slaying tigers. Tippu Sultan even vented his frustration at his inability to defeat the British by ordering a special life-size toy, replete with sound, of a tiger mauling an English soldier.

At the beginning of the 20th century, the world's tiger population was estimated at 100,000, even though they had been hunted for at least a thousand years. Tigers were prized as trophies and as a source of skins for expensive coats. They were also killed on the grounds that they posed a danger to humans. As the century drew to a close, only 5,000 to 7,500 were left in the wild, and captive tigers may now outnumber wild ones. Since then, the world's tiger population has declined to about 3,500 animals. The South China tiger (*P. tigris amoyensis*) is the most endangered, with only a few dozen animals remaining. The Siberian and Sumatran subspecies number less than 500 each, and the Indo-Chinese population is estimated at about 1,500. Three subspecies have gone extinct within the past century: the Caspian (*P. tigris virgata*) of central Asia, the Javan (*P. tigris sondaica*), and the Bali (*P. tigris balica*) tigers. Because the tiger is so closely related to the lion, they can be crossbred in captivity.

Serious concern for the declining number of tigers was expressed during the latter half of the 20th century, and gradually all countries in the tiger's range took measures to protect the animal, but with varying degrees of success. The tiger is now legally protected throughout its range, but law enforcement is not universally effective. India, which accounts for half the world's tiger population, declared it the national animal and launched Project Tiger in 1973, a successful program under which selected tiger reserves received special conservation efforts and status. Nepal, Malaysia, and Indonesia have set up a string of national parks and sanctuaries where the animal is effectively protected; Thailand, Cambodia, and Vietnam are pursuing the same course. China, the only country with three subspecies of tigers, is also giving special attention to conservation. In Russia, where poaching seriously endangered the Siberian tiger, concentrated effort and effective patrolling have resulted in a revival of the subspecies.

In the 1970s tiger hunting for sport was banned in most countries where tigers lived, and the trade in tiger skins was outlawed. Nevertheless, tiger skins are still highly valued for display and for worship, as are claws, teeth, and clavicles (collarbones) for talismans. Skulls, bones, whiskers, sinews, meat, and blood have long been used by Asians, especially the Chinese, in medicines, potions, and even wine. These products are presumed to be useful in the treatment of rheumatism, rat bites, and various other diseases, for the restoration of energy, and as aphrodisiacs; whiskers are believed to cause intestinal ulcers in one's enemies. Poaching and the underground trade in tiger parts continue despite seizures and destruction of the confiscated parts.

Although poaching has been responsible for keeping the number of tigers low since the 1970s, wild tigers would still be threatened even if all poaching ceased. In countries such as India, the needs of rapidly growing human populations over the last two centuries have reduced both the quantity and the quality of habitat. Forests and grasslands so favoured by the tiger are cleared for agriculture. Reduction in prey populations results in greater dependence on livestock and the consequent retribution from man. Fortunately, the status of the tiger has aroused widespread empathy, and its cause has received substantial international support. The World Wide Fund for Nature has been a pioneer and the largest contributor, along with corporate donors and nongovernmental organizations. The Convention on International Trade in Endangered Species is entrusted with the task of controlling illegal trade in tiger derivatives.

JAGUARS

The jaguar (*Panthera onca*), also called el tigre or tigre Americano, is the largest New World member of the cat family (Felidae), once found from the U.S.-Mexican border southward to Patagonia, Arg. Its preferred habitats are usually swamps and wooded regions, but jaguars also live in scrublands and deserts. The jaguar is virtually extinct in the northern part of its original range and survives in reduced numbers only in remote areas of Central and South America; the largest known population exists in the Amazon rainforest.

Typical coloration is orange to tan, with black spots arranged in rosettes with a black spot in the centre. The jaguar resembles the leopard of Africa and Asia, but the leopard lacks the black centre spot. Along the midline of the jaguar's back is a row of long black spots that may merge into a stripe. The base colour of the jaguar varies greatly from white to black. Although brown and black jaguars appear to be solid-coloured, spots are always faintly visible.

Jaguars are also larger and more heavily built than leopards. The male jaguar, which is generally larger than the female, attains a length of 1.7 to 2.7 metres (5.6 to 9 feet), including the 60- to 90-cm (24- to 36-inch) tail, with a shoulder height of 0.7 to 0.8 metre (2.3 to 2.6 feet); it weighs from 100 to 160 kg (220 to 350 pounds). The jaguars of South America are largest.

Jaguar (Panthera onca). © Getty Images

A solitary predator, the jaguar is a stalk-and-ambush hunter; its name comes from the Indian word *yaguar,* meaning "he who kills with one leap." Jaguars are swift and agile and are very good climbers. They enter water freely and appear to enjoy bathing. Although active during the day, jaguars hunt mainly at night and on the ground. Capybara and peccary are their preferred prey, but they will also take deer, birds, crocodilians, and fish. Livestock are occasionally attacked in areas where ranches have replaced natural habitat. The cat is a savage fighter when cornered but does not normally attack humans.

Jaguars adhere to a land tenure system much like cougars and tigers. Females establish overlapping home ranges, and female offspring may inherit land from their mothers. Males establish territories twice as large as females and overlap the ranges of several females. Both sexes mark their ranges with urine. Northern populations mate toward the end of the year, but in the tropics mating activity seems not to be restricted to a particular breeding season. After a gestation period of about 100 days, the female bears one to four tiny spotted cubs weighing 100–900 grams (less than 2 pounds) that do not open their eyes for 13 days. The mother raises the young for approximately two years. Full size and sexual maturity are reached at three to four years.

The jaguar is grouped along with lions and tigers with the big, or roaring, cats and is the only such cat in the Western Hemisphere. The jaguar's sound repertoire includes snarls, growls, and deep, hoarse grunts.

LEOPARDS

The leopard (*Panthera pardus*), also called the panther, is a large cat closely related to the lion, tiger, and jaguar. Leopards were once known by the name *pard*, or *pardus*. The name *leopard* was originally given to the cat now called *cheetah*—the so-called hunting leopard—which was once thought to be a cross between the lion and the pard. The term *pard* was eventually replaced by the name *leopard*.

The leopard is found over nearly the whole of Africa south of the Sahara, in northeast Africa, and from Asia Minor through Central Asia and India to China and Manchuria. It varies greatly in size and markings. The average size is 50 to 90 kg (110 to 200 pounds) in weight, 2.1 metres (7 feet), in length excluding the 90-cm (36-inch) tail, and 60 to 70 cm (24 to 28 inches) in shoulder height. The leopard can, however, grow much larger. The ground colour is typically yellowish above and white below. Dark spots are generally arranged in rosettes over much of the body and are without the central spot characteristic of the coat of the jaguar; the ground colour within the rosettes is sometimes a darker yellow, and the size and spacing of the spots vary greatly. As a result of

Leopard (Panthera pardus). Leonard Lee Rue III

these differences in pattern, several races of leopard have been named.

The leopard is a solitary animal of the bush and forest and is mainly nocturnal in habit, although it sometimes basks in the sun. It is an agile climber and frequently stores the remains of its kills in the branches of a tree. It feeds upon any animals it can overpower, from small rodents to waterbuck, but generally preys on the smaller and medium-sized antelopes and deer; it appears to have a special liking for dogs as food and, in Africa, for baboons. It sometimes takes livestock and may attack human beings.

There is no definite breeding season; the female produces from two to four, usually three, cubs after a gestation period of about three months. The calls of the leopard vary and include a series of harsh coughs, throaty growls, and deep, purring sounds. The animal takes to water readily and is a good swimmer.

LEOPARD CATS

A leopard cat (*Felis bengalensis*) is a forest-dwelling cat found in India and Southeast Asia and noted for its leopard-like colouring. The coat of the leopard cat is usually yellowish or reddish brown above, white below, and heavily marked with dark spots and streaks. Length of the animal ranges from 45 to 75 cm (18 to 30 inches) excluding the 23- to 35-cm (9- to 14-inch) tail. The leopard cat is a nocturnal hunter, preying on birds and small mammals (including domestic fowl in some areas). It breeds in spring (possibly again later in the year in Malaysia); litters consist of two to four young, and the gestation period is about 56 days.

A black form, in which the ground colour, as well as the spots, is black, is widely known as the black panther; it is more common in East Asia than in other parts of the range of the leopard. The subspecies known as the Barbary, South Arabian, Anatolian, Amur, and Sinai leopards are considered to be endangered or critically endangered.

SNOW LEOPARDS

The snow leopard (*Panthera uncia*), also called the ounce, is a long-haired cat, family Felidae, grouped with the lion, tiger, and others as one of the big, or roaring, cats. The snow leopard inhabits the mountains of central Asia and the Indian subcontinent, ranging from an elevation of about 1,800 metres (about 6,000 feet) in the winter to about 5,500 metres (18,000 feet) in the summer. Its soft coat, consisting of a dense, insulating undercoat and a thick outercoat of hairs about 5 cm (2 inches) long, is pale grayish with dark rosettes and a dark streak along the spine. The underparts, on which the fur may be 10 cm (4 inches) long, are uniformly whitish. The snow leopard attains a length of about 2.1 metres (7 feet), including the 90-cm- (36-inch-) long tail. It stands about 0.6 metre (2 feet) high at the shoulder and weighs 23 to 41 kg (50 to 90 pounds). It hunts at night and preys on various animals, such as marmots, wild sheep, and domestic livestock. Its litters of two to four young are born after a gestation period of approximately 93 days.

Formerly classified as *Leo uncia*, the snow leopard has been placed, with the other big cats, in the genus *Panthera*. Because of certain skeletal features, it has also been separated by some authorities as the sole member of the genus *Uncia*. Genetic studies show that the common ancestor of snow leopards and tigers diverged from the lineage of big cats about 3.9 million years ago, with snow leopards branching from tigers about 3.2 million years ago. The snow leopard is listed as an endangered species in the IUCN Red List of Threatened Species.

CLOUDED LEOPARDS

Clouded leopards, also called clouded tigers, are strikingly marked cats of southeastern Asia. There are two species, which are genetically distinct from one another. *Neofelis nebulosa*, found on the mainland of southeastern Asia, particularly in forests and other wooded regions, and *N. diardi* (also called the Bornean clouded leopard), found on the islands of Sumatra and Borneo, are thought to have diverged about 1.4 million years ago. The population of clouded leopards declined sharply in the latter half of the 20th century as a result of hunting and deforestation. They are reported to be nocturnal and to live in trees; they prey on birds and on small mammals, such as pigs and monkeys.

A rather short-legged cat, the clouded leopard has a long head and large upper-canine teeth that are proportionately longer than those of any other cat. The coat of *N. nebulosa* is short and grayish brown, spotted on the body with large, dark patches partly edged with black; the head, legs, and long tail are spotted. *N. diardi* is similar in appearance but has a darker coat and smaller patches. The male clouded leopard may attain a length of about 106 cm (42 inches) excluding the 90-cm (36-inch) tail, a shoulder height of about 80 cm (32 inches), and a weight of about 23 kg (50 pounds); the female is smaller.

The clouded leopard was formerly placed in the genera *Panthera* or *Leo*, as one of the big, or roaring, cats. In other older classifications, it was considered a member of the genus *Felis*.

Cheetahs

The cheetah (*Acinonyx jubatus*) is one of the world's most recognizable cats, known especially for its speed. Cheetahs' sprints have been measured at a maximum of 114 km (71 miles) per hour, and they routinely reach velocities of 80 to 100 km (50 to 60 miles) per hour while pursuing prey. Nearly all the cheetahs remaining in the wild live in Africa.

Cheetahs are covered almost entirely with small black spots on a background of pale yellow and have a white underbelly. Their faces are distinguished by prominent black lines that curve from the inner corner of each eye to the outer corners of the mouth, like a well-worn trail of inky tears. Cheetahs have a long, slender body measuring 1.2 metres (4 feet), with a long tail (65 to 85 cm [26 to 33 inches]) that generally ends in a white tuft. They are about 75 cm (2.5 feet) tall at the shoulder. Weight ranges from 34 to 54 kg (75 to 119 pounds), males being slightly larger than females.

Natural History

Cheetahs have evolved many adaptations that enhance their ability to sprint. Their legs are proportionally longer

Cheetah (Acinonyx jubatus). Leonard Lee Rue III

than those of other big cats; an elongated spine increases stride length at high speeds; they have unretractable claws, special paw pads for extra traction, and a long tail for balance. Internally, the liver, adrenal glands, lungs, bronchi, nasal passages, and heart are all large to allow intense physiological activity. During a chase, cheetahs take about 3½ strides per second and 60 to 150 breaths per minute. Chases are usually limited to sprints of less than 200 to 300 metres, however, because the increased physiological activity associated with running creates heat faster than it can be released through evaporative cooling (sweating through their paws and panting).

Unlike most carnivores, cheetahs are active mainly during the day, hunting in the early morning and late afternoon. A cheetah eats a variety of small animals, including game birds, rabbits, small antelopes (including the springbok, impala, and gazelle), young warthogs, and larger antelopes (such as the kudu, hartebeest, oryx, and roan). Prey is generally consumed quickly to avoid losing it to competitors such as lions, leopards, jackals, and hyenas.

Cheetahs inhabit a wide variety of habitats, including the dry, open country and grasslands where they are most often seen, as well as areas of denser vegetation and rocky upland terrain. Groups consist of a mother and her young or of coalitions made up of two or three males that are often brothers. Adult males and females rarely meet except to mate. Male coalitions live and hunt together for life and occupy an area that may overlap the range of several adult females. Female home ranges are generally much larger than those of male coalitions.

Following a gestation period of three months, the female gives birth to two to eight cubs, usually in an isolated spot hidden in the cover of tall grass or thicker vegetation. At birth, cubs weigh about 250 to 300 grams (slightly more than half a pound). Their fur is dark and includes a thick yellowish gray mane along the back, a trait that presumably offers better camouflage and increased protection from high temperatures during the day and low temperatures at night during the first few months of life. Mortality among young cubs can be as high as 90 percent in the wild, often because of other predators. The mother leaves her offspring when they are 16 to 24 months old. Young males are chased away by the resident male coalition, traveling several hundred kilometres before establishing residence and becoming sexually active at 2½ to 3 years of age. Female offspring will generally inhabit the same vicinity as their mother. Life expectancy of cheetahs is about 7 years in the wild and generally from 8 to 12 years in captivity.

Status and Taxonomy

The cheetah has lived in association with humans since at least 3000 bc, when the Sumerians depicted a leashed cheetah with a hood on its head on an official seal. During this period in Egypt, the cheetah was revered as a symbol of royalty in the form of the cat goddess Mafdet. Cheetahs were kept as pets by many famous historical figures, such as Genghis Khan, Charlemagne, and Akbar the Great of India (who had more than 9,000 in his stable). These cats were also used for sport. Trained and tame, they were typically hooded and carried on horseback or in a cart, then dehooded and released near their quarry. In spite of the large numbers of cheetahs kept in captivity by royalty during the 14th to 16th centuries, almost all were captured from the wild because there was essentially no captive breeding. Because of this continuous drain on wild Asiatic populations, cheetahs from Africa were being imported into India and Iran during the early 1900s.

In 1900 an estimated 100,000 cheetahs were found in habitats throughout continental Africa and from the Middle East and the Arabian Peninsula to India. Today cheetahs have been extirpated from a large portion of this area. In Asia they are nearly extinct, with the largest confirmed population (a few dozen) inhabiting northeastern Iran. In Africa there are an estimated 9,000 to 12,000 cheetahs, with the largest populations existing in Namibia, Botswana, and Zimbabwe in Southern Africa and Kenya and Tanzania in East Africa. Smaller, more isolated populations exist in other countries, including South Africa, Congo (Kinshasa), Zambia, Somalia, Ethiopia, Mali, Niger, Cameroon, Chad, and the Central African Republic. All populations are threatened, even within protected areas, because of increased competition from large predators such as lions and hyenas. Outside of reserves, humans pose a threat in several forms, including habitat loss, poaching, and indiscriminate trapping and shooting to protect livestock.

The cheetah was common throughout North America, Europe, and Asia until the end of the last ice age, about 10,000 years ago—a time coincident to when large numbers of mammals disappeared throughout the Northern Hemisphere. All North American and European cheetahs and most of those in Asia vanished. About this time the cheetah populations seem to have experienced what may have been the first and most severe of a series of size reductions (demographic bottlenecks). Modern cheetahs retain evidence of this historic event in their DNA. There is a very high level of genetic similarity in all but the most rapidly evolving parts of the cheetah's genome, which makes all of today's individuals appear highly inbred. This condition has been linked with increased susceptibility to infectious diseases (such as feline infectious peritonitis, or FIP), increased infant mortality, and high levels of abnormal sperm. No evidence, however, links low levels of genetic variation with reduced fitness in wild populations.

Early taxonomists interpreted the numerous specialized traits of cheetahs as evidence that they diverged from the other cat species early in the evolutionary history of the cat family (Felidae). The cheetah was therefore granted unique taxonomic status, and since the early 1900s it has been classified as the only species of genus *Acinonyx*. Cheetahs are often divided into five subspecies: *A. jubatus jubatus* in Southern Africa, *A. jubatus fearsoni* (including *A. jubatus velox* and *A. jubatus raineyi*) from eastern Africa, *A. jubatus soemmeringii* from Nigeria to Somalia, *A. jubatus hecki* from northwestern Africa, and *A. jubatus venaticus* from Arabia to central India. The king cheetah, once thought to be a distinct subspecies, is a Southern African form that has a "blotchy" coat pattern presumably from a rare recessive genetic mutation.

Numerous molecular genetic studies suggest that the cheetah shares a common ancestor with the puma and jaguarundi, from which it diverged six to eight million years ago, probably in North America. Fossils attributable to cheetahlike species dating from two to three million years ago have been found in North America in what is now Texas, Nevada, and Wyoming.

PUMAS

The puma (*Puma concolor*), also called the mountain lion, cougar, panther (in the eastern U.S.), or (formerly) catamount, is a large brownish New World cat comparable in size to the jaguar—the only other large cat of the Western Hemisphere. The puma has the widest distribution of any New World mammal, with a range extending from southeastern Alaska to southern Argentina and Chile. Pumas live in a variety of habitats, including desert scrub, chaparral, swamps, and forests, but they avoid agricultural areas, flatlands, and other habitats lacking cover (vegetative or topographic).

Pumas living near the Equator are generally smaller than those living farther north and south. Males in North America average 62 kg (136 pounds), but rare individuals can exceed 100 kg (220 pounds); length is about 1.2 metres (4 feet), excluding the 75-cm (30-inch) tail. Females are somewhat shorter and average about 42 kg. The specific name *concolor* ("of one colour") refers to the puma's fur, which is uniformly brown on the back, sides, limbs, and tail. The shade of brown varies geographically and seasonally from gray to reddish brown, and some black pumas have been reported; facial colour patterns are also variable. The underside is lighter. The long tail is commonly tipped with black and usually held close to the ground when the puma is walking.

The puma is active mostly at dusk, night, and dawn. Throughout its range its primary prey is hoofed mammals (ungulates, especially deer) larger than itself. In North America each puma kills about 48 ungulates per year and a larger number of smaller prey, including rabbits and hares, coyotes, bobcats, porcupines, beavers, opossums, raccoons, skunks, and other pumas. Domestic livestock, especially sheep, goats, and young calves, are also taken. It is rare for pumas to feed on carcasses that they did not kill. When hunting, a puma moves about 10 km (6 miles) per night, hunting in several travel bouts averaging 1.2 hours each. Traveling alternates with shorter periods of stalking, waiting in ambush, or resting. Slower than most of its prey, it springs from cover at close range, usually from behind the intended victim. When feeding on a large mammal, it minimizes spoilage and loss to scavengers by dragging the carcass to a secluded cache site and covering it with leaves and debris. During the day the cat commonly beds within 50 metres of the carcass, and it will feed for an average of three nights on a large kill. Except when feeding on large prey, a puma rarely beds in the same location on successive days.

Adult males and females are both solitary except for breeding associations lasting one to six days. Pumas are usually silent, but during this time they emit long, frightening screams intermittently for several hours. Pumas breed throughout the year, with a summer peak in births at higher latitudes. The interval between births is about two years, but it is less if a litter dies or disperses early. Cubs are born after a 90-day gestation period; the litter size usually is three but ranges from one to six. Spotted and born blind, each weighs about half a kilogram. The birth site, usually in nearly impenetrable vegetation, is kept free of feces and prey remains. It lacks any obvious modifications and is abandoned when the cubs are about 40 to 70 days old. Cubs are reared without assistance from adult males, which occasionally kill cubs that are not their own offspring. Cubs accompany their mother until dispersing at 10 to 26 months of age, but most die before they can fend for themselves. Upon surviving their first two years, juvenile females disperse 10 to 140 km (6 to 87 miles), averaging 32 km (20 miles); juvenile males generally disperse farther, sometimes traveling more than 250 km (155 miles). It may take a year for them to become part of the breeding population, and during the transition an individual may sequentially occupy and abandon one to five small transient home ranges. If a home range can be established, the cat can be expected to live another 7 to 11 years. Wolves and bears occasionally kill pumas and sometimes commandeer the carcasses of prey killed by them. Most deaths, however, are attributable to hunters, other cougars, or motor vehicles.

Pumas live at low density (one to five per 100 square km, or every 40 square miles) and thus, in order to survive, require large areas with sufficient prey and cover from which to ambush it. In a given region there are about two adult females for every male. There is extensive overlap between female home ranges but very little overlap between territories of adjacent males. Home ranges vary greatly in size, but the average female territory is 140 square km (54 square miles), with male territories being about twice as large.

STATUS AND TAXONOMY

At the time of European settlement in the New World, pumas occupied all of what are today the lower 48 United States and southern Canada. At present, they are primarily found west of 100° W longitude (approximately central Texas to Saskatchewan) except for southern Texas and are an endangered population in Florida (the Florida panther, *Puma concolor coryi*). Information is lacking for Central and South America, although most suitable habitats there are thought to be inhabited.

Since 1950 pumas have been eliminated from the states of Arkansas, Louisiana, Tennessee, and West Virginia. Until the 1960s pumas were taken by U.S. government hunters and subject to state bounties. Since 1970 control efforts in the United States and Canada have focused on known livestock killers, and most states and provinces now manage populations for sustained sport hunting. In

Florida panther (Puma concolor coryi). Courtesy, Stuart L. Pimm

THE WWF

The World Wide Fund for Nature is an international organization committed to conservation of the environment. In North America it is called the World Wildlife Fund.

In 1960 a group of British naturalists—most notably biologist Sir Julian Huxley, artist and conservationist Peter Scott, and ornithologists Guy Mountfort and Max Nicholson—led an effort to establish an organization that protected endangered species and their habitats. The following year the World Wildlife Fund was founded; the international name was subsequently changed to World Wide Fund for Nature in 1989, although in the United States and Canada it retained the founding name. The organization's distinctive panda logo was created by Scott. In the face of growing environmental threats over the ensuing years, the WWF's activities expanded in scope. Today its mission statement is threefold: to conserve the world's biological diversity, to ensure that the use of renewable natural resources is sustainable, and to promote the reduction of pollution and of wasteful consumption. The organization has long included both conservationists and businesspeople with the intention of combining solid scientific data with well-managed action. It also seeks cooperation between nongovernmental organizations, local governments, and local populations. The WWF works closely with the World Conservation Union and has formed partnerships with the United Nations, the World Bank, and the European Union.

The WWF provides money for conservation initiatives around the world. These include programs focused on individual species, forests, and freshwater and marine issues as well as climate change and responsible international trade. The group has also been involved in efforts to provide a safe and sustainable habitat for the world's peoples, both urban and rural, including clean water, clean air, healthful food, and rewarding recreation areas. Among the WWF's notable achievements is its use of debt-for-nature swaps, in which an organization buys some of a country's foreign debt at a discount, converts the money to local currency, and then uses it to finance conservation efforts. The WWF's first successful debt-for-nature swap took place in 1987 in Ecuador.

At the beginning of the 21st century, the WWF was active in more than 100 countries and had more than five million supporters. The organization's international headquarters are in Gland, Switz., and it has more than 90 offices around the world.

most of the western United States and Canada, populations are thought to be stable or increasing except where habitat is being fragmented by urban sprawl.

Although cougars are elusive and usually avoid people, there are about four attacks and one fatality per year on humans in the United States and Canada. Most victims are children or adults traveling alone. Risk can be minimized by walking in groups and keeping children within sight. An aggressive human response can avert an impending attack and can repel an attack in progress.

The power and stealth of the puma have come to epitomize the wilderness, and the cat has therefore received prominent consideration in conservation and recovery efforts. For example, habitat corridors are planned between large natural areas in order to benefit large carnivores such as the puma. Research has demonstrated that dispersing pumas readily find and use habitat corridors, and radio tracking of these wide-ranging predators can be used to identify appropriate areas to conserve as corridors.

Puma concolor is the only species of the genus *Puma*, although there are more than a dozen recognized races throughout the New World. Until 1995 pumas were classified in the genus *Felis*, which formerly included many much-smaller and less-vocal cats but not the jaguar (*Panthera onca*). The name *puma* is a native Peruvian term.

SMALLER WILD FELINES

Around the world can be found a host of felines that, though smaller than the big cats, are just as formidable within their own ecological niches. These range from the lynxes of North America and Eurasia to the fishing cats of South and Southeast Asia.

BOBCATS

The bobcat (*Lynx rufus*), also called the bay lynx or wildcat, is a bobtailed North American cat (family Felidae), found from southern Canada to southern Mexico. The bobcat is a close relative of the somewhat larger Canada lynx (*Lynx canadensis*).

A long-legged cat with large paws, a rather short body, and tufted ears, the bobcat is 60 to 100 cm (24 to 40 inches) long, excluding the 10- to 20-cm (4- to 8-inch) tail, stands 50 to 60 cm (20 to 24 inches) at the shoulder, and weighs 7 to 15 kg (15 to 33 pounds). Its fur, stiffer and less valuable than that of the lynx, is pale brown to reddish with black spots. The underparts are white; the tip of the tail is black above, white below.

Sometimes found in suburban areas, the bobcat is a nocturnal, generally solitary cat equally at home in forests

*Bobcat (*Lynx rufus*). Joe Van Wormer/Photo Researchers*

and deserts; it is less inclined than the lynx to climb trees or swim. It feeds on rodents, rabbits, hares, and some birds. Breeding takes place in spring (sometimes a second time later in the year); a litter of one to six kittens is born after a gestation period of about 50 days. Economically, the bobcat is of some value as a furbearer and is important in keeping the numbers of rodents and rabbits under control.

CARACALS

The caracal (*Felis caracal*), also called the desert lynx or Persian lynx, is a short-tailed cat (family Felidae) found in hills, deserts, and plains of Africa, the Middle East, and central and southwestern Asia. The caracal is a sleek, short-haired cat with a reddish brown coat and long tufts of black hairs on the tips of its pointed ears. Long legged and short tailed, it stands 40 to 45 cm (16 to 18 inches) at the shoulder and varies from 66 to 76 cm (26 to 30 inches) in length excluding its 20- to 25-cm (8- to 10-inch) tail. The swift caracal is generally solitary and nocturnal in habit. It preys on birds and mammals, such as gazelles, hares, and peafowl. In Asia, where it has become rare, it has been trained as a hunting animal. The female bears litters of one to four young, which resemble the adults. The caracal sometimes is given the scientific name *Lynx caracal* or *Caracal caracal*.

FISHING CATS

The fishing cat (*Felis viverrina*) is a tropical cat of the family Felidae, found in India and Southeast Asia. The coat of the fishing cat is pale gray to deep brownish gray and marked with dark spots and streaks. The adult animal stands about 40 cm (16 inches) at the shoulder, weighs 8 to 11 kg (18 to 24 pounds), and is from 60 to 85 cm (24 to 34 inches) long, excluding the black-ringed tail, which accounts for an additional 25 to 30 cm. The fishing cat lives near water and in jungles, reed beds, and marshes. It is reported to fish by scooping its prey out of the water.

FLAT-HEADED CATS

The flat-headed cat (*Felis planiceps*) is an extremely rare Asian cat found in the Malay Peninsula, Sumatra, and Borneo. One of the smallest members of the cat family, Felidae, the adult is from 40 to 60 cm (16 to 24 inches) long without the 15- to 20-cm (6- to 8-inch) tail and weighs from 1.5 to 2.5 kg (3.3 to 5.5 pounds). Its coat is reddish above and white with red spots below; there are white markings around the eyes. It is the only feline known to include any substantial amount of vegetation in its diet, with a preference for fruit and, when available, sweet potatoes and similar foods. Little else is known about this cat, which is reported to be nocturnal and to hunt fish and frogs along rivers.

GEOFFROY'S CATS

Geoffrey's cat (*Oncifelis geoffroyi*) is a South American cat of the family Felidae, found in mountainous regions, especially in Argentina. It is gray or brown with black markings and grows to a length of about 90 cm (36 inches), including a tail of about 40 cm (16 inches). Geoffroy's cat climbs well and preys on small mammals and birds. It breeds once a year; litters consist of two or three kittens.

GOLDEN CATS

The golden cat is either of two cats of the family Felidae: the African golden cat (*Felis aurata*), or the Asian golden cat (*F. temmincki*), also known as Temminck's cat.

The African golden cat is a solitary, nocturnal inhabitant of tropical forests. It is 90–100 cm (36–40 inches) long, including the 20- to 25-cm (8- to 10-inch) tail, and stands about 40 cm (16 inches) at the shoulder. The coat is either solid reddish brown or grayish brown above, and white with dark spots below.

The Asian golden cat, also a forest dweller, is found in India and Southeast Asia. Its coat is typically an unmarked, deep, reddish brown above and paler below, with white and black markings on the face. Its colour varies, however, and may be brown or grayish; in China the coat is reported to have dark markings. The adult cat measures from 75 to 85 cm (30 to 34 inches) long, excluding the 40- to 48-cm

Asian golden cat (Felis temmincki). Russ Kinne—Photo Researchers

(16- to 19-inch) tail. It preys on birds and small mammals and reportedly bears its litters of two or three young in hollow trees or other secluded den sites.

JAGUARUNDIS

The jaguarundi (*Felis yagouaroundi*), also spelled jagua-rondi, is a small, unspotted New World cat (family Felidae) that is also known as the otter-cat because of its otterlike appearance and swimming ability. The jaguarundi is native to forested and brushy regions, especially those near water, from South America to the southwestern United States; it is, however, very rare north of Mexico.

A sleek, long-bodied animal, it has small ears, short legs, and a long tail. The adult measures from 90 to 130 cm (36 to 52 inches) in length, including the 30- to 60-cm (12- to 24-inch) tail; stands 25 to 30 cm (10 to 12 inches) at the shoulder; and weighs from 4.5 to 9 kg (10 to 20 pounds). There are two colour varieties of the jaguarundi: a reddish brown form, known as the eyra, and a gray form. Kittens of both varieties may appear in one litter.

The jaguarundi lives alone and may be active at any time of day or night. It preys on birds and small mammals. Breeding takes place at the end of the year, and a litter

THE LIGER

The offspring of a lion and a tigress, the liger is a zoo-bred hybrid—as is the tigon, the result of mating a tiger with a lioness. It is probable that neither the liger nor the tigon occurs in the wild, as differences in the behaviour and habitat of the lion and tiger make interbreeding unlikely. The liger and the tigon possess features of both parents, in variable proportions, but are generally larger and darker than either. It is thought that most, if not all, male ligers and tigons are sterile; the females, however, on occasion, may be able to produce young.

of two or three young is born after a gestation period of about 63 days.

LYNXES

The lynx (*Lynx*) is any of several short-tailed cats (family Felidae), found in the forests of Europe, Asia, and northern North America.

The Canada lynx (*Lynx canadensis*) and the bobcat (*L. rufus*; described above) live in North America. The Eurasian lynx (*L. lynx*) and the Iberian lynx (*L. pardinus*) are their European counterparts. The Iberian lynx is the most endangered feline; fewer than 200 individuals remain in the mountainous scrubland of southern Spain.

Lynx are long-legged, large-pawed cats with tufted ears, hairy soles, and a broad, short head. The coat, which forms a bushy ruff on the neck, is tawny to cream in colour and somewhat mottled with brown and black; the tail tip and ear tufts are black. In winter the fur is dense and soft, up to 10 cm (4 inches) long, and is sought by humans for trimming garments. Lynx range in size from 80 to 100 cm (32 to 40 inches) long, without the 10- to 20-cm (4- to 8-inch) tail, and stand about 60 cm (24 inches) at the shoulder. Weight is from 10 to 20 kg (22 to 44 pounds).

Nocturnal and silent except during the mating season, lynx live alone or in small groups. They climb and swim well and feed on birds and small mammals. The Eurasian lynx will take larger prey such as deer. The Canada lynx depends heavily on the snowshoe hare for food, and its population increases and decreases regularly every 9 or 10 years, relative to the population of its prey. Devastation of the Iberian lynx's staple prey— the European rabbit (*Oryctolagus cuniculus*)—by several

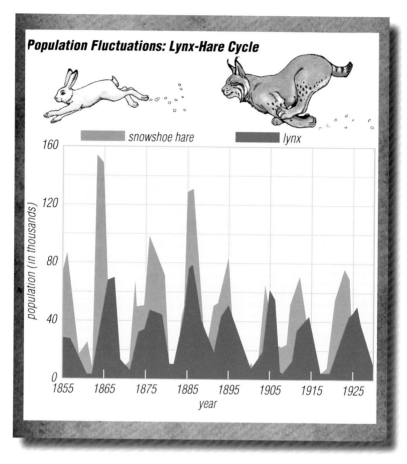

Population Fluctuations: Lynx-Hare Cycle

Cyclic fluctuations in the population density of the snowshoe hare (Lepus americanus) *and its effect on the population of a predator, the Canada lynx* (Lynx canadensis). *The graph is based on data derived from the records of the Hudson's Bay Company.* Encyclopædia Britannica, Inc.

epidemics beginning in the 1950s, as well as sensitivity to human disturbance, has been responsible for major reductions in the feline's numbers, though captive breeding and monitoring programs have had limited success in halting the cat's decline.

Lynx breed in late winter or early spring, and a litter of one to four young is born after a gestation period of about two months.

MARBLED CATS

The marbled cat (*Felis marmorata*) is a rare Southeast Asian cat (family Felidae) that is often referred to as a miniature version of the unrelated clouded leopard. The marbled cat is about the size of a domestic cat; it measures roughly 45 to 60 cm (18 to 24 inches) long, excluding a tail of approximately the same length. The coat is long, soft, and pale brown to brownish gray, with large, dark-edged blotches on the body and smaller dark spots on the legs and tail. The marbled cat is nocturnal and lives in jungles, and may feed on small animals and birds.

MARGAYS

The margay (*Leopardus wiedii*), also called the tiger cat or tigrillo, is a small cat (family Felidae) that ranges from South through Central America and, rarely, into the extreme southern United States. Little is known about the habits of the margay. It lives in forests and presumably is nocturnal, feeding on small prey such as birds, frogs, and insects. It is largely arboreal and has specially adapted claws and feet that enable it to scamper up tree

Margay (Leopardus wiedii). John H. Gerard—The National Audubon Society Collection/Photo Researchers

trunks and along branches with ease. The margay resembles the related ocelot but has a longer tail and fuller face, emphasized by large, dark eyes and rounded ears. The male attains a maximum length of about 1.1 metres (3.5 feet), including a tail about 46 cm (18 inches) long, and weighs up to about 16 kg (35 pounds). The female is generally smaller and has a relatively longer tail. Coloration varies from pale gray to deep brown with dark markings such as spots, stripes, bands, and black-edged blotches. When hand-reared from a kitten, the margay reportedly is easily tamed; as an adult, however, it may become unpredictable.

OCELOTS

The ocelot (*Felis*, or *Leopardus, pardalis*) is a spotted cat of the New World, found in lowland areas from Texas southward to northern Argentina. The short, smooth fur is patterned with elongated, black-edged spots that are arranged in chainlike bands. The cat's upper parts vary

The ocelot is a wild cat that lives in parts of North and South America. Encyclopædia Britannica, Inc.

in colour from light or tawny yellow to gray. There are small black spots on the head, two black stripes on each cheek, and four or five black stripes along the neck. The ocelot's underparts are whitish, spotted with black, and the tail is marked on the upper surface with dark bars or blotches.

Though larger than domestic cats, ocelots are small compared to jaguars. Adults measure about 70 to 90 cm (28 to 35 inches) long, not including the tail, and stand about 45 cm (18 inches) at the shoulder. They weigh 11 to 16 kg (24 to 35 pounds), with females being generally smaller than males.

The ocelot is considered terrestrial but also climbs well, inhabiting tropical forests, grasslands, or brush-covered regions. Its traces can be seen as fine scratch marks on fallen logs and as tracks in fresh mud. Ocelots tend to be silent and adapt well to disturbed habitats; thus, they sometimes live near villages. They hunt chiefly at night, feeding upon rodents, birds, reptiles, invertebrates, and fish. Ocelots sometimes move about during the day, keeping themselves hidden in undergrowth, but may rest in more open sites beneath treefalls or among the buttress roots of trees.

Breeding is not believed to be seasonal, and the gestation period is 70 days. A litter usually contains two or three young that are darker than adults but have a similar coat pattern. The kittens are sheltered in a den and are cared for by the mother.

Frequently maintained in captivity, the ocelot is one of the most commonly seen of the spotted cats. However, because they have long been hunted for their skins, they can be rare in many areas. In fact, the ocelot population is declining throughout most of its range, and one scrubland subspecies, the Texas ocelot (*F. p. albescens*), is endangered. The hunting of ocelots and the trading of their pelts are prohibited in the United States and most other countries in the animal's range.

The margay and the oncilla closely resemble the ocelot in general appearance and range, but the ocelot is larger and has a tail that is shorter than its hind leg. Until recently, these cats were all considered members of the same genus as domestic cats (*Felis*). DNA studies now indicate that these cats and some other New World species are of a different lineage within the cat family, Felidae.

PALLAS'S CATS

The Pallas's cat (*Felis manul*), also called the steppe cat or manul, is a small, long-haired cat (family Felidae) native to deserts and rocky, mountainous regions from Tibet to Siberia. It was named for the naturalist Peter Simon Pallas. The Pallas's cat is a soft-furred animal about the size of a house cat and is pale silvery gray or light brown in colour. The end of its tail is ringed and tipped with black, and some individuals have vague, dark markings on the body. The fur of the underparts is about twice as long as that of the upperparts and possibly represents an adaptation to the cat's habitual lying and crouching on cold ground.

Head and body length ranges from 45 to 60 cm (18 to 24 inches) with an additional 23 to 30 cm (9 to 12 inches) for the tail; weight ranges from 2.5 to 3.5 kg (5.5 to 7.7 pounds). The Pallas's cat is distinguished by a broad head with high-set eyes and low-set ears. It has been suggested that the positioning of these features is an adaptation for peering over rocky ledges; the supposition is that the cat thus exposes only a small part of itself to its prey of small mammals (such as pikas and rodents) and birds.

Serval (Felis serval). Christina Loke/Photo Researchers

SERVALS

The serval (*Felis serval*) is a long-limbed cat, family
Felidae, found in Africa south of the Sahara, especially in
grass- and bush-covered country near water. A swift, agile
cat, the serval climbs and leaps very well. It is a nocturnal hunter preying on birds and small mammals such as
rodents and hares.

The serval is a slender cat with a long neck, small head,
and large, slightly cupped ears. The adult is 80 to 100 cm
(32 to 40 inches) long, the tail accounting for an additional
20 to 30 cm (8 to 12 inches). It stands about 50 cm (20
inches) at the shoulder and weighs about 15 kg (33 pounds).
The coat is typically long and whitish on the underparts
and yellowish to reddish brown above, liberally marked
with black spots and stripes. These bold markings are
replaced by smaller spots or specks on some individuals,

which are known as servaline cats and were once considered a distinct species (*Felis brachyura* or *servalina*). All-black individuals are found in some populations, especially those from the high country of Kenya.

The female serval normally bears a litter of two to four kittens; the gestation period has been given as 68 to 74 days.

WILDCATS

The wildcat (*Felis silvestris*) is a small wild member of the cat family (Felidae) native to Eurasia. The name *wildcat* is also used as a general term for feral domestic cats and for any of the smaller wild species of the cat family, such as the lynx or bobcat.

The European wildcat inhabits forested regions from Scotland through continental Europe to western Asia. It is similar to the domestic cat but has longer legs, a larger,

Wildcat (Felis silvestris). Philip Wayre/EB Inc.

flatter head, and a full, relatively short tail ending in a rounded (not pointed) tip. The coat is yellowish gray with dark stripes and bands in the striped tabby pattern; the tail is black-ringed. The adult wildcat is 50 to 80 cm (20 to 32 inches) long, excluding a 25- to 35-cm (10- to 14-inch) tail; it stands 35 to 40 cm (14 to 16 inches) high at the shoulder and weighs from 3 to 10 kg (6.6 to 22 pounds).

The European wildcat is a solitary, nocturnal animal that preys on birds and small mammals and is reported to raid farms, stealing poultry and lambs. It breeds once yearly (in spring) in continental Europe and twice (sometimes three times) yearly in Scotland. A litter consists of three to six kittens; the gestation period is 68 days. The wildcat interbreeds with the domestic cat. Certain authorities believe that the purity of the Scottish wildcat (one of the several races) is being threatened by interbreeding.

CHAPTER 5

WEASELS AND THEIR RELATIVES

W easels are small carnivores with long, flexible bodies, flattened heads, and short limbs. They and their relatives — the ferrets, polecats, badgers, martens, and otters, the wolverine, and other similar animals — are gathered into the weasel family, Mustelidae, which contains as many as 54 species. Mustelids inhabit terrestrial and aquatic regions throughout the world, except Australia, Antarctica, and most oceanic islands. Many,

Stone marten (Martes foina). Reinhard/Reiser—Bavaria-Verlag

such as the American mink (*Mustela vison*), are trapped or raised commercially for their pelts.

The otters, 13 species of lithe and slender aquatic mammals, are members of Mustelidae that live in freshwater and marine environments. This chapter focuses on the terrestrial mustelids.

NATURAL HISTORY OF THE MUSTELIDS

Most mustelids are fairly small. The least weasel (*Mustela nivalis*), which measures 11 to 26 cm (4 to 10 inches) long and weighs only 25 grams (0.9 ounce), is the smallest. The largest is the sea otter (*Enhydra lutris*) at about 1 metre (3.3 feet) long and a weight of 25 to 45 kg (55 to 99 pounds). The largest terrestrial mustelid is the wolverine (*Gulo*

Wolverine (Gulo gulo). Alan G. Nelson/Root Resources

gulo), found in the northern United States and throughout Canada and northern Europe. It measures up to 1.2
metres (4 feet) in length and can weigh up to 20 kg (45
pounds) or more.

Many mustelids have a long tube-shaped body, short
legs, and a strong, thick neck with a small head. All possess
well-developed anal scent glands. The five digits on each
foot are equipped with sharp nonretractile claws. Males
are usually larger than females; among some weasels males
are almost twice as large. A tubular body does not retain
heat as well as a stockier body of the same weight and is
therefore associated with higher metabolism. As a result,
mustelids are very active and inquisitive in their constant
search for prey.

Most mustelids are strictly carnivorous, but a few
include plant matter—mostly fruits or berries—in their
diet. Dentition is characterized by strong canine teeth
and sharp molars and premolars. Some mustelids have specialized diets. Clawless otters (genus *Aonyx*) specialize on
crustaceans (especially crabs) and mollusks, whereas other
otters (genus *Lutra*) are primarily fish eaters. Specialization
even occurs between sexes in the weasels (genus *Mustela*),
in which males consume larger prey than females owing to
their larger size.

Mustelids are mostly solitary except for Eurasian
badgers (*Meles meles*), sea otters (*Enhydra lutris*), and some
northern river otters (*Lontra canadensis*). In solitary species, association between males and females during the
mating season is brief. Mating occurs mostly in the spring,
and in many species ovulation is induced during copulation. Delayed implantation of the fertilized egg occurs in
many mustelids. Females raise the young alone. Only the
least weasel produces two litters yearly; other species produce annually. In most mustelids, young become sexually

mature at about 10 months of age. Mustelids evolved from North American and Eurasian forms in the early Oligocene Epoch, some 30 million years ago.

WELL-KNOWN MUSTELIDS

From the weasel to the mink to the wolverine, several members of Mustelidae are commonly known for their size, their bold and predatory nature, or the luxuriousness of their pelts.

WEASELS

A weasel is any of various small carnivores with very elongated, slender bodies. Most live in the Northern Hemisphere and belong to the genus *Mustela*, which in addition to weasels proper includes 16 species of ferrets and polecats as well as the mink and the ermine. Along

Long-tailed weasel (Mustela frenata). John H. Gerard

with their tubelike bodies, weasels have small, flattened heads, long, flexible necks, and short limbs. The fur is short but dense, and the slim tail is pointed at the tip. Five toes on each foot end in sharp, curved claws. The species can be differentiated by size, colour, and relative length of the tail.

Weasels are usually brown with white or yellowish underparts. In winter the coats of weasels living in cold regions turn white. Their pelts, especially that of the stoat (*M. erminea*), are known as ermine in the fur trade. The kolinsky (kolinski), also called the Siberian weasel (*M. sibirica*), is also much valued for its fur. The tail hairs are used to make artists' paintbrushes.

Weasels are bold and aggressive predators. They generally hunt alone, feeding principally on mice, voles, rats, and rabbits, but they also take frogs, birds, and bird eggs. Because of their narrow bodies, weasels are able to pursue and capture rodents in their burrows and to chase them through holes and crevices, under dense herbage, up trees, or into water. Although proficient at catching mice, weasels are also notorious for raiding chicken coops. Because they cannot accumulate fat and thus must eat frequently, weasels often kill more prey than they can immediately consume and will store excess food for later use. This explains the carnage often seen after they discover captive domestic fowl.

Male weasels mate with multiple females and do not provide parental care. Most species have a single litter per year, but the common, or least, weasel (*M. nivalis*) often has two. Sexual maturity is rapidly attained, and least weasels often breed at three months of age. Litter size varies from three to a dozen or more in some species. The young are born after a gestation period of anywhere from 35 days to more than 10 months, the latter because of delayed implantation of the fertilized egg.

The most common and widely distributed species are the stoat (called the short-tailed weasel in North America) and the least weasel. The range of both extends into polar regions. The stoat was introduced into New Zealand to control rabbits, but instead it became troublesome and now endangers many of the country's native birds. The least weasel is the smallest living carnivore; the smallest subspecies inhabits North America. It measures 11 to 26 cm (4 to 10 inches) in length and weighs only 25 grams (0.9 ounce). Larger forms of the same species occur in Russia and adjacent countries, where they are somewhat longer and considerably heavier. The range of the stoat and the least weasel overlap, and in these areas the species can be differentiated by the stoat's black-tipped tail. In North America the largest weasel is the long-tailed weasel (*M. frenata*); in South America it is the tropical weasel (*M. africana*). Both measure 25 to 30 cm (10 to 12 inches), excluding the 10- to 20-cm (4- to 8-inch) tail; weight is 85 to 350 grams (3 to 12 ounces). With most weasels, males are usually twice the size of females.

Weasels belong to the family Mustelidae, and there are three weasel genera in addition to *Mustela*. The Patagonian weasel (*Lyncodon patagonicus*) is a larger mustelid of the South American Pampas. It is about 30 to 35 cm (12 to 14 inches) long, excluding the 6- to 9-cm (2.5- to 3.5-inch) tail. This weasel is grayish with dark brown underparts and a white stripe running across the forehead to the sides of the neck. The zorilles, or African striped polecats (two species of the genus *Ictonyx*), are somewhat smaller and are often found in agricultural areas. Their bodies are spotted black-and-white, and the tail, face, and back are striped. The African striped weasel (*Poecilogale albinucha*) is found in Africa south of the Congo Basin. Similar in habit to weasels of the genus *Mustela*, it is striped in light yellow and black, with black underparts and a long white tail.

BADGERS

Badger is a common name for any of several stout carnivores, most of them members of the weasel family (Mustelidae), that are found in various parts of the world and are known for their burrowing ability. The 10 species differ in size, habitat, and coloration, but all are nocturnal and possess anal scent glands, powerful jaws, and large, heavy claws on their forefeet, which are used to dig for food and construct underground dens. The North American badger (*Taxidea taxus*) feeds mostly on rodents, but Old World species are omnivorous. Badgers are

North American badger (Taxidea taxus). Alvin E. Staffan—The National Audubon Society Collection/Photo Researchers

classified into six genera. Some, especially the American badger, are hunted for their pelts.

The American badger, the only New World species, is usually found in open, dry country of western North America. Muscular, short-necked, and flat-bodied, it has a broad, flattened head and short legs and tail. The colour of the coat is grayish and grizzled, dark at the face and feet with a white stripe extending from the nose to the back. It is 23 cm (9 inches) tall and 42 to 76 cm (17 to 30 inches) long, excluding the 10- to 16-cm (4- to 6-inch) tail, and it weighs 4 to 12 kg (9 to 26 pounds). The American badger is a powerful animal that captures most of its prey by rapid digging. Generally solitary, it feeds mainly on rodents, particularly ground squirrels, pocket gophers, mice, and voles. Other prey include insects, reptiles, and eggs of ground-nesting birds. Mostly nocturnal, American badgers spend the day inside a burrow often dug the night before. Home ranges are from 1 to 10 square km (0.4 to 4 square miles), depending on habitat and food resources. During the winter they sleep underground for long periods. To survive this period of fasting, they accumulate large amounts of body fat during late summer and autumn. Mating occurs during this time, but implantation of the zygote is delayed. Thus, although the young (usually two or three) are born the following spring, true gestation is only six weeks.

The Eurasian badger (*Meles meles*) is omnivorous, consuming earthworms, insects, small mammals, birds and their eggs, and also fruits and nuts. It is grayish, with large black-and-white facial stripes. It is 30 cm (12 inches) tall and 56 to 81 cm (22 to 32 inches) long, excluding the 12- to 20-cm (5- to 8-inch) tail, and weighs 8 to 10 kg (18 to 22 pounds) or more. This social species lives in groups within an extensive network of burrows called sets. Adult Eurasian badgers have few natural predators. In

Europe tuberculosis and starvation are the most important causes of natural mortality, but thousands are killed annually by vehicles.

Ferret badgers (genus *Melogale*), also called tree badgers or pahmi, consist of four species: Chinese (*M. moschata*), Burmese (*M. personata*), Everett's (*M. everetti*), and Javan (*M. orientalis*). They live in grasslands and forests from northeast India to central China and Southeast Asia where they consume mostly insects, worms, small birds, rodents, and wild fruits. They are brownish to blackish gray, with white markings on the face, throat, and sometimes the back. Smaller than American and Eurasian badgers, they average 33 to 43 cm (13 to 17 inches) long, excluding the 12- to 23-cm (5- to 9-inch) tail.

The hog badger (*Arctonyx collaris*), also called the hog-nosed, or sand, badger, is a pale-clawed species of both lowland and mountainous regions in a range similar to that of ferret badgers. It is gray to black, with a black-and-white-striped head pattern and white throat, ears, and tail. It is 55 to 70 cm (22 to 28 inches) long, excluding the 12- to 20-cm (5- to 8-inch) tail, and weighs 7 to 14 kg (15 to 30 pounds). Hog badgers are nocturnal and find food by rooting. Their diet consists mostly of earthworms and other invertebrates, but they also consume fruits and small mammals.

FERRETS

A ferret, also called a fitchet, is either of two species of carnivore, the common ferret and the black-footed ferret, belonging to the weasel family (Mustelidae).

THE COMMON FERRET

The common ferret (*Mustela putorius furo*) is a domesticated form of the European polecat, which it resembles in size and habits and with which it interbreeds. The common ferret differs in having yellowish white (sometimes brown) fur and pinkish red eyes. The common ferret is also slightly smaller than the polecat, averaging 51 cm (20 inches) in length, including the 13-cm (5-inch) tail. It weighs about 1 kg (2 pounds).

Ferrets are popular pets and are commonly used in veterinary research. In captivity they become tame and playful and remain inquisitive. Although ferrets are adaptable, their dependence on humans becomes such that they are unable to survive without care and if lost often die within a few days. Ferrets can subsist on a diet of water and meat similar to that given the domestic cat. Easily bred in captivity, females bear two litters of six or seven young each year. Because common ferrets are subject to foot rot, their cages must be kept scrupulously clean.

Ferreting, the use of ferrets to drive rabbits, rats, and other vermin from their underground burrows, has been practiced since Roman times in Europe and even longer in Asia. In the case of rabbits, for example, a ferret is released into rabbit burrows to flush them into waiting nets or traps. The ferret's long tubular body and short limbs, as well as its aggressive hunting, make it ideal for this function.

The Black-Footed Ferret

The black-footed ferret (*Mustela nigripes*) of the American Great Plains is an endangered species. The black-footed ferret resembles the common ferret in colour but has a black mask across the eyes and brownish black markings on the feet and the tail's tip. It weighs a kilogram or less, males being slightly larger than females. Body length is 38 to 50 cm (15 to 20 inches), with a tail 11 to 15 cm (4 to 6 inches).

Black-footed ferrets live in prairie-dog burrows and eat only prairie dogs, both as prey and as carrion. They were originally found living among prairie-dog populations ranging from southern Canada through the American West to northern Mexico. As prairie dogs were largely eliminated by the development of agriculture in the Great Plains, ferrets very nearly went extinct. By 1987 the last members of a remaining population of 18 animals were captured from the wild in Wyoming. A captive breeding program was begun, and since 1991 groups have been reintroduced to native habitats in Wyoming, Montana, South Dakota, Arizona, Colorado, Utah, and Chihuahua state, Mexico. The success of the reintroduction program ultimately will depend on the preservation of prairie-dog habitats.

Black-footed ferrets are solitary except during the breeding season in March and April. Births occur in May and June, and females raise the young (kits) alone. Three kits are the norm, but litters range from one to six. Young are born in a modified burrow and emerge in July to become independent in September or October, at which time the young, especially males, usually disperse. Sexual maturity is attained after a year. Longevity in the wild is not known, but captive animals may live up to 12 years. Ferrets are hunted by golden eagles and great horned owls, as well as by other carnivores such as coyotes and badgers. Poisons used to control prairie dogs, especially sodium monofluoroacetate (commonly called 1080) and strychnine, probably contribute to deaths when the ferrets eat poisoned prairie dogs. Moreover, black-footed ferrets are extremely susceptible to many infectious diseases such as canine distemper. Bubonic plague can severely reduce populations of prairie dogs and thus cause food shortages for black-footed ferrets, but it is unknown whether ferrets themselves contract plague.

SABLES

A sable (*Martes zibellina*) is a graceful carnivore of the weasel family, Mustelidae, found in the forests of northern Asia and highly valued for its fine fur. The common name is sometimes also applied to related European and Asian species and to the American marten. The sable ranges from about 32 to 51 cm (13 to 20 inches) long, excluding the 13- to 18-cm (5- to 7-inch) tail, and weighs about 1 to 2 kg (2 to 4 pounds). Its body colour varies from brown to almost black, sometimes with a throat patch from dusky to salmon.

The sable is solitary and arboreal in habits, feeding on small animals and eggs. The unusually long gestation of about 250 to 300 days is caused by delayed implantation of the fertilized egg in the wall of the uterus. The litter numbers from one to four.

MINKS

The mink (*Mustela*) is either of two species of the weasel family (Mustelidae) native to the Northern Hemisphere. The European mink (*Mustela lutreola*) and the American mink (*M. vison*) are both valued for their luxurious fur. The American mink is one of the pillars of the fur industry and is raised in captivity throughout the world. In the wild, mink are small, discreet, and most often nocturnal, and they live in close proximity to water.

Both mink species measure about 30 to 50 cm (12 to 20 inches) in length, not including a 13- to 23-cm (5- to 9-inch) tail, and weigh 2 kg (4.5 pounds) or less; females are smaller. Like weasels, mink have short legs, a long, thick neck, and a broad head with short, rounded ears. The coat is deep, rich brown and sometimes has white markings on the throat, chest, and underparts. The pelage consists of a dense, soft underfur overlaid with dark and glossy guard hairs.

Wild mink are semiaquatic and obtain most of their food near the water's edge. Typically following shore-lines and banks, they investigate holes, crevices, and

American mink (Mustela vison). Karl H. Maslowski

deep water pools for hidden prey. Strictly carnivorous, mink eat mostly frogs, salamanders, fish, crayfish, musk-rats, mice, and voles, along with aquatic birds and their eggs. Occasionally, mink will search for terrestrial prey such as hares and rabbits. Mink are strong and agile swimmers and often dive to probe underwater nooks and crannies.

Mink are solitary, except during the mating season in spring. Both males and females may mate with several individuals, but females raise the young alone. Gestation typically lasts 51 days for the American mink, but this period can vary, as implantation of the fertilized egg can be delayed for 1 to 14 days. Litter size averages four young but ranges from two to eight. Young become independent after six months.

American mink raised in captivity for fur are bred during early spring, and harvest of pelts occurs when the animals reach adult size and the pelt is at maximum quality—usually during winter when mink are 6 to 8 months old. During this period, ranch mink reach sizes that may exceed twice that of wild mink because of better nutrition and selective breeding for size. Also by means of selective breeding and careful genetic follow-up, breeders can produce a wide variety of natural pelage colours, ranging from pure white to sapphire, pearl, blue, and black.

The American mink was originally found throughout North America except in the arid regions of the Southwest. The popularity of the American mink as a fur animal led to the establishment of numerous fur farms throughout the world, particularly the northern countries of North America and Eurasia. Natural disasters, poor facilities, and the voluntary and involuntary releases of captive mink (mink farms have been a frequent target of animal-rights activists) have led to the establishment of many populations of American mink far outside its native range. Today the American mink inhabits many areas of Europe, Scandinavia, Russia, South America, and even Iceland. Where introduced to the European mink's habitat, the American mink has become a problem, displacing the less aggressive and less adaptable European species, which is now rare or threatened in many parts of Europe where it was once abundant. The invasion of European waters by the American mink has also led to the decline of wetland species such as water voles and some birds.

MARTENS

A marten is any of several weasel-like carnivores of the genus *Martes* (family Mustelidae), found in Canada and parts of the United States and in the Old World from Europe to the Malay region. Differing in size and coloration according to species, they have lithe, slender bodies, short legs, rounded ears, bushy tails, and soft, thick coats that are valuable in the fur trade. Martens are forest dwelling and usually solitary; they climb easily and feed rapaciously on animals, fruit, and carrion. A litter contains one to five young; the gestation period, especially in northern areas, may last 290 days or more because of a delay before implantation of the fertilized egg in the wall of the uterus.

The best known species of *Martes* are the following:

The American marten (*M. americana*) is a North American species of northern wooded regions. It is also called pine marten; its fur is sometimes sold as American, or Hudson Bay, sable. Its adult length is 35 to 43 cm (14 to 17 inches), exclusive of the 18- to 23-cm (7- to 9-inch) tail. It weighs 1 to 2 kg (2 to 4 pounds) and has a yellowish-brown coat deepening to dark brown on tail and legs, with a pale whitish or yellowish throat patch.

The pine marten (*M. martes*) of European and Central Asian forests is also called baum marten and sweet marten. It has a dark brown coat with an undivided yellowish throat patch. Its head and body length is 42 to 52 cm (17 to 21 inches), with a 22 to 27-cm (9 to 11-inch) long tail. Its shoulder height is 15 cm (6 inches), its weight, 1 to 2 kg (about 2 to 4 pounds).

The stone marten, or beech marten (*M. foina*), inhabits wooded country in Eurasia. It has grayish-brown fur with a divided, white throat bib. It weighs 1 to 2.5 kg (2 to 5 pounds), is 42 to 48 cm (17 to 19 inches) long, and is 12 cm (5 inches) high at the shoulder.

The yellow-throated marten (*M. flavigula*), of the subgenus *Charronia*, is also called honey dog for its fondness for sweet food. It is found in southern Asia. Its head and body length is 56 to 61 cm (22 to 24 inches), and its tail is 38 to 43 cm (15 to 17 inches) long. It has a brown coat that darkens toward and on the tail, and its throat and chin are orange.

WOLVERINES

The wolverine (*Gulo gulo*), also called the glutton, carcajou, or skunk bear, is a member of the weasel family (Mustelidae) that lives in cold northern latitudes, especially in timbered areas, around the world. It resembles a small, squat, broad bear 65 to 90 cm (26 to 36 inches) long, excluding the bushy, 13- to 26-cm (5- to 10-inch) tail. Shoulder height is 36 to 45 cm (14 to 18 inches), and weight is 9 to 30 kg (20 to 66 pounds). The legs are short, somewhat bowed; the soles, hairy; the semiretractile claws, long and sharp; the ears, short; and the teeth, strong. The coarse, long-haired coat is blackish brown with a light brown stripe extending from each side of the neck along the body to the base of the tail. The animal has anal glands that secrete an unpleasant-smelling fluid.

The wolverine is noted for its strength, cunning, fearlessness, and voracity. It may follow traplines to cabins and devour food stocks or carry off portable items; its offensive odour permeates the invaded cabin. The wolverine is a solitary, nocturnal hunter, preying on all manner of game and not hesitating to attack sheep, deer, or small bears. Wolverines are also adept scavengers, and thus a large portion of their diet comes from scavenging the carcasses of elk, caribou, and other animals. No animal except humans hunts the wolverine. Its fur is valued as trimming for parkas because frost and frozen breath can easily be brushed off the smooth hairs. Solitary during most of the year, the wolverine has a short courtship in February or March. A litter contains one to five young; the female's gestation period is about nine months.

Wolverines appear to be dependent on areas of deep snowpack. Scientists studying North American wolverines have observed significant population declines in regions experiencing sharp decreases in snowpack. It is thought that harsh winters with deep snow provide more food resources for wolverines. Carcasses of deer, elk, and other ungulates are more plentiful in such conditions, and rodents—a frequent prey of wolverines found tunneling underneath deep snow—are more abundant than in snow-free conditions.

LESSER-KNOWN MUSTELIDS

Despite their usually solitary nature, many other mustelids are known and are valued either for their fur, as pets, or as objects of study. These range from the stoat of North Africa, Eurasia, and North America to the ratel of Africa and southern Asia.

ERMINES

An ermine is any of several northern weasels of the genus *Mustela,* family Mustelidae, that are called ermine especially during their winter-white colour phase. This white coat is called ermine in the fur trade.

The species that furnished the ermine for royal robes in Europe was the stoat (*M. erminea*), also called the short-tailed weasel or Bonaparte weasel. The ermine, or stoat, is found in northern North America, in Eurasia, and in North Africa. Ermines are most abundant in thickets, woodland, and semitimbered areas. These slender, agile, voracious mammals measure 13 to 29 cm (5 to 12 inches) in head and body length; have a tail length of 5 to 12 cm (2 to 5 inches); and weigh less than 0.3 kg (0.66 pound). Females are smaller than males, and northern races smaller than southern.

In summer the ermine is brown, with whitish throat, chest, and belly. In colder climates the winter coat is white, except for the black tail tip. In moderately cold climates the fur becomes only partly white.

Ermines feed on small mammals, birds, eggs, frogs, and occasional invertebrates. Small prey is seized at the base of the skull, larger prey by the throat. The litter contains 3 to 13 young, born after a gestation prolonged as much as 10 months because of delayed implantation in the wall of the uterus.

The winter-taken pelts, prized for fineness and pure colour, are among the most valuable of commercial furs and are obtained mainly in northern Eurasia. During the reign of Edward III (1327–77) of England, the wearing of ermine was restricted to members of the royal family. Thereafter, state robes were constructed in such a way that in many cases the rank and position of the wearer could be determined by the presence or absence and the disposition of the black spots.

FISHERS

Fisher (Martes pennanti). Painting by Donald C. Meighan

The fisher (*Martes pennanti*), also called the fisher marten, fisher cat, Pennant's marten, Pennant's cat, big marten, black fox, black cat, or pekan, is a rare North American carnivore of northern forests, trapped for its valuable brownish black fur (especially fine in the female). It is a member of the weasel family (Mustelidae). The fisher has a weasel-like body, bushy tail, tapered muzzle, and low, rounded ears. Adults are usually 50 to 63 cm (20 to 25 inches) long, excluding the 33- to 42-cm (13- to 17-inch) tail, and weigh 1.4 to 6.8 kg (3 to 15 pounds). Males are larger and heavier than the females. The fisher hunts both on the ground and in trees, attacking various rodents (including porcupines) and other animals. Its diet also consists of fruits and sometimes nuts. A litter contains one to five young, born after a gestation period of 338 to 358 days, including a delay before implantation of the fertilized egg in the wall of the uterus.

GRISONS

The grison, also called the huron (Spanish: "ferret"), is either of two weasel-like carnivores of the genus *Galictis* (sometimes *Grison*), family Mustelidae, found in most regions of Central and South America. Grisons are sometimes tamed when young. These animals have small, broad ears, short legs, and slender bodies 40 to 50 cm (16 to 22 inches) long, weighing 1 to 3 kg (2 to 6.5 pounds); the tail accounts for an additional 15 to 20 cm (6 to 8 inches). Their backs are grayish or brown and their limbs, lower parts, and faces are black; a white stripe runs across the forehead and along the sides of the neck. Gregarious and generally diurnal, they climb, swim, and burrow adeptly and feed on small animals and fruit. Their litters contain two to four young.

Grison (Galictis). Drawing by H. Douglas Pratt

POLECATS

A polecat is any of several weasel-like carnivores of the family Mustelidae. The pelt, especially of the European polecat, is called fitch in the fur trade.

The European, or common, polecat (*Mustela,* sometimes *Putorius, putorius*), also called the foul marten for its odour, occurs in woodlands of Eurasia and North Africa. It weighs 0.5 to 1.4 kg (1 to 3 pounds) and is 35 to 53 cm (14 to 21 inches) long exclusive of the bushy tail, which is 13 to 20 cm (5 to 8 inches) long. Its long, coarse fur is brown above, black below, and marked with yellowish patches on the face. Much lighter fur distinguishes the masked, or steppe, polecat (*M. p. eversmanni*) of Asia.

Principally terrestrial, the polecat hunts at night, feeding on small mammals and birds. It also eats snakes, lizards, frogs, fishes, and eggs. The polecat is more powerful than the marten but less active, and it rarely climbs trees. Its litters of three to eight young are born in the spring after about two months' gestation. The domestic, albino variety of the European polecat is known as the ferret.

The marbled polecat (*Vormela peregusna*) of Eurasian foothills and steppes is similar to the European species in habits, appearance, and size. It is mottled reddish brown and yellowish above, blackish below.

The zorille, a related African carnivore, is also called the striped, cape, or African polecat. In the United States the name polecat is often applied to skunks, particularly the spotted and striped species.

RATELS

The ratel (*Mellivora capensis*), also called the honey badger, is a badgerlike member of the weasel family (Mustelidae) noted for its fondness for honey. Ratels live in covered and forested regions of Africa and southern Asia. The adult stands 25 to 30 cm (10 to 12 inches) at the shoulder and has a heavily built, thick-skinned body about 60 to 77 cm (24 to 30 inches) long, plus a tail length of 20 to 30 cm (8 to 12 inches). The ears are rudimentary; the upper body parts are whitish, but the lower parts, face, and legs are black—the two colours sharply separated.

Ratels are nocturnal and live in burrows dug with their strong, incurved front claws. They feed on small

animals and fruit and on honey, which they find by following the calls of a bird, the greater, or black-throated,
honey guide (*Indicator indicator*); the ratels break open
the bees' nests to feed on the honey, and the birds in
return obtain the remains of the nest. Ratels are strong,
fearless fighters but in captivity can become tame and
playful. A litter usually consists of two cubs.

TAYRAS

The tayra (*Eira barbara*), also spelled taira, is a weasel-
like mammal of tropical forests from southern Mexico
through South America to northern Argentina. The tayra
is short-legged, yet slender and agile, weighing from 2.7
to 7 kg (5.95 to 15.4 pounds). The body, measuring about
60 to 68 cm (24 to 27 inches), is covered with coarse but
smooth, dark fur. The bushy tail is 39 to 47 cm (15 to 18.5
inches) long. The tayra's dark skin is covered by brown
or black fur that is commonly paler on the head and
neck. The throat and chest are often marked with a light-
coloured, triangular spot.

Despite their limited eyesight, tayras are skilled
climbers and have been reported to climb down smooth
tree trunks from heights of greater than 40 metres (130
feet). Active both day and night, tayras travel solo, in
pairs, or in trios on the ground and in trees; their drop-
pings can often be found on rocky outcrops. Hollow trees
or holes in the ground serve as dens. Although classified
as carnivores (order Carnivora), tayras are omnivorous,
with diets comparable to those of raccoons. Common
foods include fruits, insects, and small vertebrates as well
as eggs and carrion.

In their forest habitats, tayras often appear inquisitive,
moving their heads in an undulating, snakelike fashion to

determine scents or sights. When alarmed, tayras may snort, growl, and spit. Although seemingly playful and easily tamed from an early age, tayras make poor pets, being restless and bearing a strong odour. A typical litter is believed to contain three or four young, but, despite their wide occurrence and relatively large size, surprisingly little is known about tayra reproduction, life span, home ranges, or habits.

Tayra (Eira barbara). Drawing by H. Douglas Pratt

ZORILLES

The zorille, or zoril (*Ictonyx* [sometimes *Zorilla*] *striatus*), is an African carnivore of the weasel family (Mustelidae), frequenting diverse habitats. Also called the zorilla, striped polecat, African polecat, or Cape polecat, it has a slender body, 29 to 39 cm (12 to 16 inches) long, and a bushy white tail, 21 to 31 cm (8 to 12 inches) long. Its fur is long and black, white striped on the back and white spotted on the face. Usually solitary, the zorille hunts at night, feeding on rodents and insects. A typical litter contains two or three young.

CHAPTER 6

RACCOONS, SKUNKS, MONGOOSES, HYENAS, AND VIVERRIDS

Numerous small and medium-sized carnivores occupy ecological niches that have not been taken over by the large carnivores. These include the raccoons and their relatives, 18 species found only in the Western Hemisphere; the skunks, 11 species of animals found mostly in the Western Hemisphere; the 37 species of mongooses and their relatives, found mainly in Africa but also in Asia and southern Europe; the hyenas and their relatives, 4 species found in Africa and Asia; and the viverrids, 35 species found throughout the Eastern Hemisphere.

PROCYONIDS

Procyonids are members of family Procyonidae, a group of tree-climbing mammals comprising raccoons, coatis, the New World ringtail, the cacomistle, and the kinkajou. Though the 18 species of Procyonidae are classified as carnivores, procyonids are actually omnivorous and are closely related to bears (family Ursidae), a group from which they diverged about 30 to 50 million years ago. Indeed, both the giant panda (*Ailuropoda melanoleuca*) and the lesser, or red, panda (*Ailurus fulgens*) have been grouped in the past as procyonids, though they are

North American raccoon (Procyon lotor). Leonard Lee Rue III

actually bears. Procyonids are found only in the Western Hemisphere; they mostly inhabit Central America, and only the North American raccoon is widely distributed north of the tropics. The raccoon and some other procyonids are sometimes kept as pets.

KINKAJOUS

The kinkajou (*Potos flavus*), also called the honey bear, is an unusual member of the raccoon family distinguished by its long, prehensile tail, short muzzle, slender 12.7-cm (5-inch) tongue, and low-set, rounded ears. Native to Central America and parts of South America, the kinkajou is an agile denizen of the upper canopy of tropical forests.

The kinkajou is the only species of the genus *Potos*. Though related to the raccoon and coati, its appearance, behaviour, and ecology more closely resemble those of a primate. Indeed, the kinkajou was originally described to the scientific community as a lemur. It has soft, gray or brownish fur and large eyes set in a small, round face. The eyes are highly reflective of light, giving them a bright orange eyeshine. The kinkajou's feet can be rotated 180° and have a thick covering of short hair on the soles. Its body length is less than 61 cm (24 inches), excluding its 40- to 57-cm (16- to 22-inch) tail. Adult weight ranges from 2 to 3.2 kg (4.4 to 7 pounds).

Nocturnal and arboreal, kinkajous generally feed alone or in pairs but will form stable groups in which members, particularly the males, groom each other and return each morning to established tree holes to sleep together. The kinkajou is highly vocal, emitting screams, barks, and a variety of softer sounds, including some described as "sneezes." It rarely leaves the

Kinkajou (Potos flavus). Rebecca Yale/ Flickr/Getty Images

trees, feeding mostly on fruit and insects; it also drinks nectar from flowers during dry periods. A litter consists of one or two young, born in spring or summer.

The kinkajou often shows little fear of humans. It is sometimes kept as a pet known as a "honey bear," although the animal cannot be litter-trained. Considered gentle if they are obtained when young, kinkajous do possess anal glands that produce a musky odour when the animal is angered or frightened; kinkajous can also deliver a sharp bite. In captivity, they can live 20 years or more.

NATURAL HISTORY OF THE PROCYONIDS

Procyonids are relatively small carnivores that usually weigh 1 to 12 kg (2 to 26 pounds), depending on the species. Body lengths range from 30 to 70 cm (12 to 28 inches), and tails range from 20 to 70 cm (8 to 28 inches). Coats are generally brown, and many species have facial markings and a dark-banded tail. The eyes are large and the ears rounded. The tail can be prehensile, as in the kinkajou (*Potos flavus*), or semiprehensile and used for balance, as in the coatis (genera *Nasua* and *Nasuella*). The feet have five digits and are void of fur on the soles. Long fingers allow great dexterity; all species are good climbers, and at least one species, the kinkajou, is arboreal. The claws are short, curved, and either nonretractile or semiretractile. Like bears, procyonids walk on the soles of the feet (plantigrade locomotion), leaving clear imprints of the paw pad and all digits. Procyonids have 40 teeth, with long canine teeth and small, sharp premolars; the molars are broad. This dentition is indicative of an omnivorous diet that includes animal flesh, invertebrates, fruits, and grains. Kinkajous are mostly fruit eaters (frugivorous), whereas other species are opportunistic and consume whatever is available.

OLINGOS

The olingo (genus *Bassaricyon*), also called the cuataquil, is any of about four species of small arboreal carnivores of the raccoon family, Procyonidae, found in the jungles of Central and northern South America. Olingos are slender, grayish-brown animals 35 to 50 cm (14 to 20 inches) long, excluding the bushy, faintly ringed tail, which accounts for an additional 40 to 50 cm (16 to 20 inches). They have soft fur, pointed muzzles, and rounded ears. They resemble kinkajous but are less stocky and have narrower snouts and longer-haired, nonprehensile tails. Olingos are nocturnal, often travel in small groups, and feed primarily on fruit. Little else is known of their habits.

Social systems of procyonids vary. There are the extensive groupings of unrelated animals observed in coatis, the family groups of raccoons, and creatures that are solitary, such as the kinkajou. Males mate with more than one female, and most procyoinids breed in the spring. Young are often born in hollow trees, tree cavities, or abandoned farm buildings. Only females provide parental care. Except for kinkajous, procyonids do not defend territories, with the result that many animals can occupy a relatively small area. Densities are affected mostly by abundance of food, depredation by humans, and natural predation and disease. The highest densities of procyonids occur among raccoons inhabiting urban areas of North America, such as Toronto in Canada and Chicago in the United States.

RACCOONS

Raccoons (*Procyon*), also called ringtails, are any of seven species of nocturnal mammals characterized by bushy, ringed tails. The most common and well-known is the North American raccoon (*Procyon lotor*), which ranges from northern Canada and most of the United States southward into South America. It has a conspicuous black "mask" across the eyes, and the tail is ringed with five to ten black bands.

A stout animal with short legs, a pointed muzzle, and small erect ears, the North American raccoon is 75 to 90 cm (30 to 36 inches) long, including the 25-cm (10-inch) tail. Weight is usually about 10 kg (22 pounds) or less, although large males may grow to more than 20 kg (44 pounds). Those living in northern regions are larger than their southern counterparts. The North American raccoon's fur is shaggy and coarse, and its colour is iron-gray to blackish with brown overtones. Southern raccoons are typically more silver, with northern "coons" tending toward blond or brown.

Like all raccoons, the North American raccoon is an intelligent and inquisitive animal. The hairless front feet are highly dexterous and resemble slender human hands, the hind feet being thicker and longer. Although classified as a carnivore, the raccoon is omnivorous, feeding on crayfish and other arthropods, rodents, frogs, and fruit and other plant matter, including crops. Raccoons are mistakenly believed to "wash" their food before eating it if water is available. This misconception arises from their habit of searching for food in or near water and then manipulating it while eating.

Raccoons adapt extremely well to human presence, even in towns and cities, where they den in buildings and thrive on a diet of garbage, pet food, and other items available to them. As availability of food is the primary factor affecting the abundance of raccoons, the highest population densities are often found in large cities. In the wild raccoons live in a wide variety of forest and grassland habitats. Most often found in proximity to water, they are also proficient swimmers. They climb readily and usually den in riverbanks, hollow trees or logs, or abandoned beaver lodges.

Raccoons overcome winter food shortages by becoming dormant. This period may last from a few days, in response to occasional southern cold spells, to four to six months at northern latitudes. Northern raccoons are able to do this by accumulating large amounts of body fat during the late summer and autumn. Most will double their springtime body weight in order to provide themselves with enough energy to sleep through the winter.

In early spring males mate with more than one female. Annual litters contain one to six (usually three or four) young, born in late spring after a gestation period of 60 to 73 days. The female takes a keen interest in her young and cares for them for about a year, even though the young begin hunting food and are weaned at about two months. In captivity raccoons can live up to 20 years, but few survive beyond 5 in the wild. Their large size and vigorous defense sometimes enable them to fend off predators such as bobcats, coyotes, and mountain lions. Most deaths, however, are caused by humans and disease, especially canine distemper, parvovirus, and rabies. Rabies is especially significant in the eastern United States, where raccoons surpassed skunks in 1997 as the most frequent vector of the disease. Vaccine-laden bait has been air-dropped in Canada in an effort to stop the spread of rabies.

Because of its fondness for eggs, nestlings, corn, melons, and garbage, the raccoon is unwelcome in some areas. It is still hunted (often with hounds) and trapped for its fur and flesh. The North American raccoon played an important role in the North American fur industry during the 19th century. In the early decades of the 20th century, raccoon coats were de rigueur for the sporting set. As a result of the fur's value, raccoons were introduced to France, the Netherlands, Germany, and Russia, where they have become a nuisance. In the latter portion of the 20th century, raccoons expanded their range northward in Canada, likely because of conversion of forest to agricultural land. Warmer temperatures and less-severe winters would enable raccoons to extend their range even farther.

The crab-eating raccoon (*P. cancrivorus*) inhabits South America as far south as northern Argentina. It resembles the North American raccoon but has shorter, coarser fur. The other members of genus *Procyon* are not well known. Most are tropical and probably rare. They are the Barbados raccoon (*P. gloveralleni*), the Tres Marías raccoon (*P. insularis*), the Bahaman raccoon (*P. maynardi*), the Guadeloupe raccoon (*P. minor*), and the Cozumel raccoon (*P. pygmaeus*).

CACOMISTLES

Cacomistles, or cacomixls (*Bassaris cus*), are either of two species of large-eyed, long-tailed carnivores related to the raccoon (family Procyonidae). Cacomistles are grayish brown with lighter underparts and white patches over their eyes. The total length is about 60 to 100 cm (24 to 40 inches), about half of which is the bushy, black-and-white-ringed tail. The animals weigh about 1 kg (2.2 pounds) and have small faces with long ears and pointed snouts. They are arboreal and nocturnal and feed on a variety of small animals, fruit, and vegetation. The gestation period is about 51 to 54 days, and litters contain from one to five (usually three or four) young.

The species *B. astutus,* widely known as miner's cat, ringtailed cat, or ringtail, is found in rocky areas from the southwestern United States to southern Mexico. It is an agile animal with rounded ears and semiretractile claws. It is sometimes kept as a pet and is an excellent mouser. The species *B.* (formerly *Jentinkia*) *sumichrasti* ranges in forests from Central America to Peru. Larger, darker-furred, and more arboreal than the ringtail, it has pointed ears and nonretractile claws.

COATIS

Coatis (genus *Nasua*), also called coatimundis or coatimondis, are any of three species of omnivore related to raccoons (family Procyonidae). Coatis are found in wooded regions from the southwestern United States through South America.

The coati has a long, flexible snout and a slender, darkly banded tail that it often carries erect as it moves about. It has coarse fur that is gray to reddish or brown with lighter underparts and light facial markings. The male coati measures about 73 to 136 cm (29 to 54 inches) in length—half of which is tail—and weighs roughly 4.5 to 11 kg (10 to 24 pounds). The female is somewhat smaller.

Female and young coatis commonly live in bands of 5 to 40 and travel together. The males are solitary and join the bands only during the short mating season of approximately a month. The gestation period is about 77 days long, and litters usually consist of two to six young.

Coatis are most active during the day. Like their raccoon relatives, they are curious and resourceful creatures and are good climbers. When foraging, they comb the trees as well as the ground for seeds, fruits, eggs, and a wide variety of small animals ranging from insects to mice.

SKUNKS

Skunks, also called polecats, are black-and-white mammals of the family Mephitidae, found primarily in the Western Hemisphere, that use extremely well-developed scent glands to release a noxious odour in defense. The term *skunk* refers to more than just the well-known striped skunk (*Mephitis mephitis*). The skunk family is composed of 11 species, 9 of which are found in the Western Hemisphere. Primarily nocturnal, skunks are diverse

Striped skunk (Mephitis mephitis). E.R. Degginger

carnivores that live in a wide variety of habitats, including deserts, forests, and mountains. Most are about the size of a house cat, but some are significantly smaller.

The common striped skunk is found from central Canada southward throughout the United States to northern Mexico. Its fur is typically black with a white "V" down the back, and it has a white bar between the eyes, as does the rare hooded skunk (*M. macroura*) of the southwestern United States. In the hooded skunk stripes are not always present, and white areas on the back are interspersed with black fur, which gives it a gray appearance. The "hood" is the result of long hairs at the back of the neck.

Spotted skunks (genus *Spilogale*) live from southwestern Canada to Costa Rica. Except for a white spot between the eyes, their spots are actually a series of interrupted stripes running down the back and sides. These are about the size of a tree squirrel and are the smallest skunks except for the pygmy spotted skunk (*S. pygmaea*), which can fit in a person's hand.

The hog-nosed skunks (genus *Conepatus*) of North America can be larger than striped skunks, but those of Chile and Argentina are smaller. In the northern part of their range, they have a single solid white stripe starting at the top of the head that covers the tail and back. In Central and South America they have the typical "V" pattern. Hog-nosed skunks have no markings between the eyes.

In the 1990s stink badgers (genus *Mydaus*) became classified as members of the family Mephitidae, and they thus are now considered skunks. Found only in the Philippines, Malaysia, and Indonesia, they resemble small North American hog-nosed skunks with shorter tails. Their white stripes can be divided, single and narrow, or absent. Stink badgers consist of two species, the Malayan stink badger (*Mydaus javanensis*), also called the skunk badger or teledu, and the Palawan, or Calamanian, stink badger (*M. marchei*). The Malayan stink badger is an island dweller of Southeast Asia that usually lives in mountainous areas. It is brown to black with white on the head and sometimes with a stripe on the back. It is 38 to 51 cm (15 to 20 inches) long, excluding the short tail, and weighs 1 to 4 kg (about 2 to 8 pounds). The Palawan stink badger is a little-known badger from the Philippines on Palawan and neighbouring islands. Its scent is very strong and offensive. Like skunks, stink badgers have anal glands that produce a strong-smelling fluid that can be sprayed.

SCENT

Skunk scent comes from anal glands located inside the rectum at the base of the tail. All carnivores have anal scent glands, but they are extremely well-developed in skunks. Each of the two glands has a nipple associated with it, and skunks can aim the spray with highly coordinated muscle control. When a skunk is being chased by a predator but cannot see it, the spray is emitted as an atomized cloud that the pursuer must run through. This usually is enough to deter most predators. When the skunk has a target to focus on, the spray is emitted as a stream directed at the predator's face. Although accurate to about two metres (more than six feet), its total range is considerably farther.

A skunk will go through a series of threat behaviours before it sprays. Striped and hooded skunks will face an adversary head-on and stamp their front paws, sometimes charging forward a few paces or edging backward while dragging their front paws. When they actually spray, they can simultaneously face their head and tail at the antagonist. Hog-nosed skunks stand up on their hind paws and slam their front paws to the ground while hissing loudly. Spotted skunks perform a handstand and approach predators. Stink badgers snarl, show their teeth, and stamp their forefeet. They also have been observed to feign death, with the anal area directed at the observer. The chemical composition of skunk spray differs among species, but sulfur compounds (thiols and thioacetates) are primarily responsible for its strength.

Natural History

Hog-nosed skunks are capable diggers and have powerfully built upper bodies, which allow them to climb in rough terrain. Spotted skunks are the most agile, able to climb in squirrel-like fashion both up and down trees. Striped skunks spend most of their time on the ground and are less agile than spotted skunks. Striped skunks are omnivorous, feasting on insects, small vertebrates, and eggs, as well as vegetable matter. Hog-nosed skunks and stink badgers have elongated snouts adapted to rooting for grubs and other insects in the soil; they too rely on a variety of foods. Spotted skunks are the most carnivorous.

Skunks remain solitary except during breeding season, though in colder climates females may den together. After mating, the male is driven off, and the female raises the litter of 2 to 12 offspring (kits) alone. Kits are born from about the end of April through early June. Breeding occurs in the spring, except in the Western spotted skunk (*S. gracilis*), which breeds in the autumn but undergoes a period of delayed implantation lasting about 150 days. Eastern spotted skunks (*S. putorius*) breed at the same time of year as other skunks, which results in both species' producing litters at the same time.

Striped skunks are common throughout their range, but population estimates for other species are uncertain. The Eastern spotted skunk may be on the decline throughout its range, but no skunks are listed as endangered species. Despite their unique system of defense, they are eaten, chiefly by great horned owls but also by eagles, crows, vultures, coyotes, foxes, dogs, bobcats, mountain lions, American badgers, and even humans. Stink badgers are preyed upon by civets, cats, and humans. Automobiles are a major cause of mortality for skunks in the United States.

IMPORTANCE TO HUMANS

Skunk pelts (especially striped) were once valuable in the fur industry but are less so today. Living skunks are more valuable, as most prey primarily on insects, especially those harmful to agriculture. They are also very useful in destroying rats and mice that commonly infest farm buildings. Spotted skunks are particularly efficient hunters because they are quick and are able to follow rodents into smaller spaces than can larger skunks. The earliest legislation for the protection of skunks was passed in 1894 and grew out of appeals from hop growers in New York. In some areas of North America, skunks are a major carrier of rabies, which is fatal to skunks. Striped skunks can be tamed but do not generally make good pets.

PALEONTOLOGY

Skunks have long been classified as a subfamily of the weasel family (Mustelidae). Genetic data, however, suggest placement of skunks in their own family, Mephitidae (*mephitis* being Latin for "bad odour"). The oldest fossil identified as a skunk dates to 11 to 12 million years ago and was discovered in Germany. Genetic data indicate the family originated about 30 to 40 million years ago. Stink badgers were formerly included in the badger subfamily of the Mustelidae, but comparative anatomy and genetic data were used to reclassify them with skunks.

MONGOOSES AND MEERKATS

Mongooses and meerkats are small, bold, predatory carnivores that make up the family Herpestidae and are found mainly in Africa but also in southern Asia and southern Europe. There are 37 species belonging to 18 genera. The most common and probably best-known are the 10 species of the genus *Herpestes*, among which are the Egyptian mongoose, or ichneumon (*H. ichneumon*), of Africa and southern Europe and the Indian gray mongoose (*H. edwardsii*), made famous as Rikki-tikki-tavi in Rudyard Kipling's *The Jungle Books* (1894 and 1895). The meerkat (*Suricata suricata*) is also a member of the mongoose family.

Meerkats and the other mongooses were formerly included within Viverridae, a very old carnivore family that includes civets and genets. However, most mongooses differ from viverrids by being terrestrial, insectivorous, diurnal, and gregarious. The presence of an anal scent gland and associated sac further differentiates mongooses from members of Viverridae.

MONGOOSES

Mongooses (also known as mongeese) are short-legged animals with pointed noses, small ears, and long, furry tails. The claws are nonretractile, and in most species there are five toes on each foot. The fur is gray to brown and is commonly grizzled or flecked with lighter gray. Markings, when present, include stripes, dark legs, and pale or ringed tails. The adult size varies considerably, with the smallest being the dwarf mongoose (*Helogale parvula*), which measures 17–24 cm (7–10 inches) with a 15–20-cm tail.

Mongooses live in burrows and feed on small mammals, birds, reptiles, eggs, and occasionally fruit. A number of mongooses, including those of the genus *Herpestes*, will attack and kill poisonous snakes, such as king cobras. They depend on speed and agility, darting at the head of the snake and cracking the skull with a powerful bite. They are not immune to venom, as popularly believed, nor do they seek and eat an herbal remedy if bitten. A number of species are noted for the unusual manner in which they open eggs and other food items with hard shells (such as crabs, mollusks, nuts). The animal stands on its hind legs and hits the egg against the ground. Sometimes it carries the egg to a rock and, standing with its back to the rock, throws the egg between its legs and against the rock until the shell is broken. Early reports of this behaviour met with skepticism but have been verified by other observers. The Madagascar narrow-striped mongoose (*Mungotictis decemlineata*) exhibits the same behaviour but lies on its side and uses all four feet to toss the egg.

Most species are active during the day and are terrestrial, although the marsh mongoose (*Atilax paludinosus*) and a few others are semiaquatic. Some mongooses live alone or in pairs, but others, such as the banded mongoose (*Mungos mungo*) and dwarf mongooses (genus *Helogale*), live in large groups. Litters usually consist of two to four young.

Some species, mainly the Javan mongoose (*Herpestes javanicus*) but also the Indian gray mongoose, were introduced to numerous islands, including Mafia Island (off the coast of East Africa), Mauritius, numerous islands in the Adriatic Sea off the coast of Croatia, Hawaii, and the Fiji islands. Originally intended to help control rodents and snakes, these introductions were disastrous, because the mongooses severely depleted the populations of native fauna. Because of the potential destructiveness of the animals, importation of all mongooses into the United States is strictly regulated.

MEERKATS

The meerkat, or mierkat (*Suricata suricatta*), is a burrowing member of the mongoose family (Herpestidae), found in southwestern Africa, that is unmistakably recognizable in its upright "sentinel" posture as it watches for predators. The meerkat is slender and has a pointed little face, tiny ears, and black eye patches. Body length is about 29 cm (11 inches), and the smooth, pointed tail is 19 cm (8 inches) long. Colour varies from dark to grizzled light gray or tan, with broad dark bars across the back and a black-tipped tail. Adults weigh less than 1 kg (2.2 pounds), with older dominant breeders heavier than subordinates. Easily tamed, the meerkat is sometimes kept as a pet to kill rodents.

Also called the suricate, meerkats live in cooperative packs of 3 to 25 with partially overlapping home ranges of a few square kilometres, which they mark with secretions

Meerkat, or suricate (Suricata suricatta). © Gordon Langsbury/Bruce Coleman Ltd.

of the anal glands. Packs will chase or fight one another if they meet. Meerkats shelter in burrow systems having multiple entrances and measuring up to 5 metres (16 feet) across. Several levels of tunnels and chambers extend to 1.5 metres (5 feet) below ground. Each home range contains about five such warrens. Packs spend the night inside, and pups are born there. They also retreat into their tunnels for an afternoon rest to avoid the heat of midday. While the temperature may be 38 °C (100 °F) on the surface, it is 23 °C (73 °F) a metre below. Meerkats probably dig these warrens themselves, although they have been reported to move in with South African ground squirrels (*Xerus inauris*).

In the morning the pack leaves the den to search for food—mostly beetles, caterpillars, termites, spiders, and scorpions but also lizards, birds, small snakes, and rodents. They forage five to eight hours per day, spaced one to five metres apart while softly vocalizing to maintain contact. Prey is located in crevices and under stones or logs primarily by smell and is rapidly dug up. Large prey is battered with the heavy claws on the forefeet before being torn to pieces. In the dry season meerkats obtain water by digging up succulent tubers.

As they forage in broad daylight in the open and away from the den, meerkats are susceptible to attack, especially by jackals and raptors. While digging, they glance around frequently for these predators. The prospect of being taken by surprise is met by sentinel behaviour. One meerkat takes up a raised position on a termite mound or tree branch, where it sits erect and watches. The others are aware the sentinel is on duty and can thus spend more time digging. If the sentinel sees a predator approaching, it alerts the others with a high-pitched call, and the pack scatters for cover. Pack members take turns doing this in no particular order; they do not, however, act as sentinels before they have eaten their fill, benefitting first from the early warning. Sentinels, therefore, are not really the altruists they were once thought to be.

In each pack is a dominant male that tries to prevent other males from mating. There is also a dominant female that produces more litters than other females. Meerkats are unusual among carnivores in that the pups are raised with the assistance of adults other than the parents. In the wild, a female bears one or occasionally two litters of three or four pups annually, usually during the rainy season. They are weaned at seven to nine weeks of age but are dependent on adults for much longer. Pups begin sampling insects at three weeks, but they cannot follow the adults away from the den until one or two weeks later. During this period, at least one helper each day fasts while it keeps the pups inside the den and defends against neighbouring meerkats, which would kill them. Once allowed out of the den, pups follow the pack, begging with squeaks when food is dug up. Helpers feed pups until they are three to six months old and carry pups that fall behind when the pack moves. They even crouch over the pups, shielding them from attack by raptors. Helpers are thus valuable to the breeding female but less so if there are other litters to care for. For that reason, the dominant female is extremely hostile to subordinates that try to breed, and she causes endocrine effects that prevent young females from ovulating. If this fails, the dominant female may attack subordinates during estrus and pregnancy or kill their pups. Pups are also killed by subordinates, a fact apparently recognized by the dominant female. She expels other females late in her own pregnancy. About half of those expelled return a few weeks later, when her hostility has subsided. The dominant one's ability to control other females is reduced in a large pack, particularly as subordinate females reach the age of three years. Births among other mothers become more common, and the pack consists of several family groups living cooperatively, though the dominant female still produces more pups than all her subordinates combined. Apparently, it is so hazardous for meerkats to leave the larger pack, and so unlikely that they could rear offspring without helpers anyway, that many young animals simply postpone reproduction. In the meantime, they raise others' pups in order to maintain larger pack size, as individuals in large packs live longer. Small packs do not survive drought years, possibly because they are expelled from their home ranges by larger neighbouring packs.

As a tunneler, the meerkat is possibly the most specialized mongoose. The narrow feet have four toes instead of five and possess extremely long, tough nails on the forefeet. The animal also has smaller ears and thinner hair. The yellow mongoose (*Cynictis penicillata*), sometimes called the red meerkat, is intermediate in form between meerkats and other mongooses, and at times will share warrens with meerkats. The yellow mongoose has four toes on the hind feet but five on the forefeet, larger ears, and a bushy coat and tail.

HYENAS AND AARDWOLVES

Hyenas, or hyaenas, are any of three species of coarse-furred, doglike carnivores of family Hyaenidae found in Asia and Africa and noted for their scavenging habits. Hyenas have long forelegs and a powerful neck and shoulders for dismembering and carrying prey. Hyenas are tireless trotters with excellent sight, hearing, and smell for locating carrion, and they are proficient hunters as well. All hyenas are more or less nocturnal.

Hyena. Liquidlibrary/Jupiterimages

Although hyenas look like dogs, they are actually more closely related to cats. Order Carnivora branched into dog and cat lineages 50 million years ago, and hyenas arose from the cat group about 30 million years ago. Early hyaenids did not all have bone-crushing molars; those were probably a recent development as some hyenas exploited large carcasses left by sabre-toothed cats.

Hyaenidae also includes the aardwolf, which looks like a small striped hyena. It has a specialized diet of insects and belongs to a subfamily separate from hyenas (though some authorities place it in a family of its own called Protelidae).

Hyenas

Intelligent, curious, and opportunistic in matters of diet, hyenas frequently come into contact with humans. The spotted, or laughing, hyena (*Crocuta crocuta*) is the largest species and will burglarize food stores, steal livestock, occasionally kill people, and consume wastes—habits for which they are usually despised, even by the nomadic Masai of East Africa, who leave out their dead for hyenas. Even so, hyena body parts are sought for traditional tokens and potions made to cure barrenness, grant wisdom, and enable the blind to find their way around. Brown hyenas (*Parahyaena brunnea* or sometimes *Hyaena brunnea*) are blamed for many livestock deaths that they probably do not cause. Similarly, from North Africa eastward to India, striped hyenas (*H. hyaena*) are blamed when small children disappear and for supposedly attacking small livestock and digging up graves. In consequence, some hyena populations have been persecuted nearly to extinction. All three species are in decline outside protected areas.

Spotted hyenas range south of the Sahara except in rainforests. They are ginger-coloured with patterns of dark spots unique to each individual, and females are larger than males. Weighing up to 82 kg (180 pounds), they can measure almost 2 metres (6.6 feet) long and about 1 metre (3.3 feet) tall at the shoulder. Spotted hyenas communicate using moans, yells, giggles, and whoops, and these sounds may carry several kilometres. Gestation is about 110 days, and annual litter size is usually two cubs, born in any month.

The spotted hyena hunts everything from young hippos to fish, though antelopes are more common. In East and Southern Africa, they kill most of their own food, chasing wildebeest, gazelles, and zebras at up to 65 km per hour for 3 km (40 miles per hour for 2 miles). Contrary to popular belief, healthy as well as weakened individuals are taken. One or two animals may start the chase, but dozens might be in on the kill; an adult zebra mare and her two-year-old foal (370 kg [810 pounds] total weight) were observed being torn apart and consumed by 35 hyenas in half an hour. Strong jaws and broad molars allow the animal to get at every part of a carcass and crush bones, which are digested in the stomach by highly concentrated hydrochloric acid. Spotted hyenas sometimes go several days between meals, as the stomach can hold 14.5 kg (32 pounds) of meat.

Living in clans of 5 to 80 individuals, spotted hyenas mark the boundaries of their territory with dung piles ("latrines") and scent from anal glands. Females' genitals externally resemble males' and have social importance in the genital greeting, in which animals lift the hind leg to allow for mutual inspection. The sexes have a linear dominance hierarchy, the lowest female outranking the highest male. The dominant female monopolizes carcasses when she can, which results in better nutrition for her cubs. The dominant male obtains most matings. For 6 months a cub's only food is mother's milk; nursing bouts may last four hours. Where prey is migratory, the mother "commutes" 30 km or more from the den, and she may not see her cubs for three days. After 6 months the cubs begin eating meat from kills, but they continue to drink milk until 14 months old. Female cubs inherit the status of their mothers; young males sometimes move to other clans, where they are more likely to breed.

The smaller brown hyena weighs about 40 kg (90 pounds); the coat is shaggy and dark with an erectile white mane over the neck and shoulders and horizontal white bands on the legs. The brown hyena lives in Southern Africa and western coastal deserts, where it is called the beach, or strand, wolf. Birds and their eggs, insects, and fruit are staples, but leftovers from kills made by lions, cheetahs, and spotted hyenas are very important seasonally. Small mammals and reptiles are occasionally killed. After 3 months' gestation, cubs (usually three) are born anytime during the year and are weaned by 15 months of age. Like spotted hyenas, brown hyenas live in clans that mark and defend territory, but behaviour differs in several critical ways: adult females nurse each other's cubs; other clan members take food to the cubs; and females do not outrank males.

Five races of striped hyenas live in scrub woodland as well as in arid and semiarid open country from Morocco to Egypt and Tanzania, Asia Minor, the Arabian Peninsula, the Caucasus, and India. These small hyenas average 30 to 40 kg (65 to 90 pounds). Colour is pale gray with black throat fur and stripes on the body and legs. The hair is long, with a crest running from behind the ears to the tail; the crest is erected to make the animal look larger. Striped hyenas apparently do not scent-mark or defend territory. Litters of one to four cubs are born any time during the year after a 3-month gestation; they are weaned at 10 to 12 months. A female's offspring may stay and help raise her new cubs. Striped hyenas have a diet much like that of brown hyenas: insects, fruit, and small vertebrates. In Israel striped hyenas are pests of melon and date crops.

AARDWOLVES

The aardwolf (*Proteles cristatus*) is an insectivorous carnivore that resembles a small striped hyena. The shy, mainly nocturnal aardwolf lives on the arid plains of Africa. There

Aardwolf (Proteles cristatus). Simon Trevor/Bruce Coleman Ltd.

are two geographically separate populations, one centred in South Africa and the other in East Africa.

The aardwolf, whose name in Afrikaans means "earth wolf," is yellowish with vertical black stripes and a bushy, black-tipped tail. Standing less than half a metre high at the shoulder, it varies in length from 55 to 80 cm (22 to 31 inches) exclusive of the 20- to 30-cm (8- to 12-inch) tail. Weight is from 8 to 12 kg (18 to 26 pounds). Like the hyena, it has a long, coarse ridge of erectile hairs along the length of the back, sturdy shoulders, and longer front than hind legs. The aardwolf, however, is less of a runner and has five toes on the front feet instead of four. The skull is not as robust, but the sharp canine teeth and strong jaws characteristic of hyenas are retained and wielded in aggressive interactions. The cheek teeth, however, are mere pegs adequate for crunching its insect diet, which consists almost exclusively of harvester termites. When the aardwolf smells termites or hears the rustle of thousands of them in the grass with its sensitive, pointed ears, it laps them up with its sticky tongue.

Although aardwolves forage alone, they live in breeding pairs that defend a territory marked by secretions from the anal glands. When attacked they may fight, and a musky-smelling fluid is emitted. Shelters can be holes, crevices, and abandoned porcupine and aardvark burrows, where usually two or three cubs are born during the rainy months, when termites are most active. Cubs are weaned by four months and have left their parents' territory by the time the next litter is born.

VIVERRIDS

Viverrids (family Viverridae) are any of 35 species of small Old World mammals including civets, genets, and linsangs. Viverrids are among the most poorly known carnivores. They are rarely encountered, being small and secretive inhabitants of forests and dense vegetation. In addition, many species live only on islands or in small areas.

Most viverrids have slender bodies with a long tail and short legs terminating in four- or five-toed feet. The neck and head are typically elongated, with a tapered muzzle and small ears. Most species have anal scent glands. Some viverrids are nocturnal, some diurnal. Many bear two annual litters of two to four young. Life expectancy ranges from 5 to 15 years.

The smallest member of the viverrid family is the spotted linsang (*Prionodon pardicolor*), which weighs 0.6 kg (1.3 pounds). The two largest species are the African civet (*Civettictis civetta*) and the fossa (*Cryptoprocta ferox*) of Madagascar, both of which can reach 20 kg (45 pounds). The most common viverrid, however, is the European genet (*Genetta genetta*), which weighs 1 to 2.5 kg (2 to 5 pounds). It is found in Spain, Portugal, France, Saudi Arabia, and Israel and throughout the savannas of Central Africa as well as most of Southern Africa.

Most viverrids are good climbers. Some, such as the fossa and the binturong (*Arctictis binturong*), spend most of their lives in trees, as do several palm civets, such as the masked palm civet (*Paguma larvata*) and the golden palm civet (*Paradoxurus zeylonensis*). Many are good swimmers, and two species, the aquatic genet (*Osbornictis piscivora*) and the otter civet (*Cynogale bennettii*), are semiaquatic. Viverrids are mostly carnivorous, their diet consisting of small rodents such as mice and voles, birds and their eggs, reptiles, amphibians, fruits, nuts, and insects. Some, such as palm civets, eat mostly fruit; their frugivorous habit is reflected in the molars, which are larger and flatter than those of carnivourous viverrids.

Viverrids rely heavily on scent for communication. In civets, perineal glands produce a secretion that is stored in a pouch and used for scent marking. Although the secretions of most civets are strong and disagreeable, those of African civets (*Civettictis civetta*) are musky and have a pleasant odour. These secretions and those of the Oriental civets (genera *Viverricula* and *Viverra*) are used in the perfume industry, and captured civets are kept specifically for the production of "civet musk." For this reason the African civet is probably the most economically important viverrid.

CIVETS

Civets, also called civet cats, are any of a number of long-bodied, short-legged carnivores of the family Viverridae. There are about 15 to 20 species, placed in 10 to 12 genera. Civets are found in Africa, southern Europe, and Asia. Rather catlike in appearance, they have thickly furred tails,

*African palm civet (*Nandinia binotata*).* Robert C. Hermes from the National Audubon Society Collection/Photo Researchers

small ears, and pointed snouts. The coloration varies widely among the species but commonly is buff or grayish with a pattern of black spots or stripes or both. Length ranges from about 40 to 85 cm (16 to 34 inches), with the tail accounting for another 13 to 66 cm (5 to 26 inches), and weight ranges from 1.5 to 11 kg (3.3 to 24 pounds). The anal glands of civets open under the tail into a large pouch in which a greasy, musklike secretion accumulates. This secretion, known as civet, is used by the animals in marking territories. The secretion of the lesser Oriental civet, or rasse (*Viverricula indica*), and of the Oriental and African civets (*Viverra*) is employed commercially in the manufacture of perfume.

Civets are usually solitary and live in tree hollows, among rocks, and in similar places, coming out to forage at night. Except for the arboreal palm civets, such as *Paradoxurus* (also known as toddy cat because of its fondness for palm juice, or "toddy") and *Nandinia* (known as the African palm civet), civets are mainly terrestrial. The otter civet (*Cynogale bennetti*), African civet (*Viverra,* sometimes *Civettictis, civetta*), and the rare Congo water civet (*Osbornictis piscivora*) are semiaquatic. Civets feed on small animals and on vegetable matter. Their litters usually consist of two or three young.

The IUCN Red List of Threatened Species lists seven civets considered to be in high risk to extremely high risk of extinction in the wild; among these are the Malabar civet (*Viverra civettina*) and the otter civet (*Cynogale bennettii*).

GENETS

Genets are any of about five species of lithe, catlike carnivores of the genus *Genetta,* family Viverridae. Genets are elongate, short-legged animals with long, tapering tails, pointed noses, large, rounded ears, and retractile claws. Coloration varies among species but usually is pale yellowish or grayish, marked with dark spots and stripes; the tail is banded black and white. Adult genets weigh 1 to 2 kg (2.2 to 4.4 pounds) and are about 40 to 60 cm (16 to 24 inches) long, excluding the 40- to 55-cm (16- to 22-inch) tail.

Except for the small-spotted genet (*G. genetta*), which also occurs in western Asia and southern Europe, they are found only in Africa. Genets live alone or in pairs and are active mainly at night. They frequent forests, grasslands, and brush and are as agile in the trees as on the ground. They prey on small mammals and birds. Litters contain two or three young.

LINSANGS

Linsangs are any of three species of long-tailed, catlike mammals belonging to the civet family (Viverridae). The African linsang (*Poiana richardsoni*), the banded linsang

BINTURONGS

The binturong (*Arctictis binturong*) is a catlike carnivore of the civet family (Viverridae), found in dense forests of southern Asia, Indonesia, and Malaysia. It has long, shaggy hair, tufted ears, and a long, bushy, prehensile tail. The colour generally is black with a sprinkling of whitish hairs. The head and body measure about 60 to 95 cm (24 to 38 inches) and the tail an additional 55 to 90 cm (22 to 35 in.); weight ranges from about 9 to 14 kg (20 to 31 pounds). The binturong is principally nocturnal and arboreal in habit, using its prehensile tail as an aid in climbing. It apparently feeds mainly on fruit but also takes eggs and small animals. In some areas it is tamed and is reported to make an affectionate pet.

(*Prionodon linsang*), and the spotted linsang (*Prionodon pardicolor*) vary in colour, but all resemble elongated cats. They grow to a length of 33 to 43 cm (13 to 17 inches), excluding a banded tail almost as long, and have slender bodies, relatively narrow heads, elongated muzzles, retractile claws, and dense, close fur.

The banded linsang occurs in Malaysia and the Indonesian archipelago, while the spotted linsang is found in tropical uplands in northern India and Myanmar (Burma), southern China, and Nepal. The African linsang, or oyan, lives in western and central Africa. All three species inhabit dense forests and jungles. The two Asian species are strictly carnivorous, but the African linsang eats plant materials as well. All three species are nocturnal and arboreal. They usually produce two litters annually, each containing two or three young.

FOSSAS

The fossa, or foussa (*Cryptoprocta ferox*), the largest carnivore native to Madagascar, is a catlike forest dweller of the civet family, Viverridae. The fossa grows to a length of

Fossa (Cryptoprocta ferox). © www.istockphoto.com / Jameson Weston

about 1.5 metres (5 feet), including a tail about 66 cm (26 inches) long, and has short legs and sharp, retractile claws. The fur is close, dense, and grayish to reddish brown. Generally most active at night, the fossa is both terrestrial and arboreal. It usually hunts alone and commonly feeds on birds and lemurs but also preys on livestock. Many legends centre on the fossa; some, such as reports of its savagery, are probably much exaggerated.

Because of certain structural features, the fossa was formerly classified in the cat family (Felidae). Its common name sometimes leads to its confusion with the Malagasy civet, or fanaloka, *Fossa fossa*.

CHAPTER 7
DOMESTIC CARNIVORES

The dog and the cat are the two most ubiquitous and popular domestic animals in the world. For more than 12,000 years, the dog has lived with humans as a hunting companion, protector, object of scorn or adoration, and friend. It is noteworthy that wolves (*Canis lupus*), the ancestors of the dog (*Canis lupus familiaris*), were social animals that lived together in packs in which there was subordination to a leader. The dog has readily transferred this allegiance from pack leader to human master. The cat (*Felis catus*), on the other hand, has not yielded as readily to subjugation. A member of the same family (Felidae) as the tiger, puma, and bobcat, the house cat shares many of their traits and is able to revert to complete self-reliance more quickly and more successfully than most domesticated dogs.

DOGS

Dogs (species *Canis lupus familiaris*) are domestic mammals of the family Canidae (order Carnivora). They are a subspecies of the gray wolf (*C. lupus*) and are related to foxes and jackals.

Dogs are regarded differently in different parts of the world. Western civilization has given the relationship between human and dog great importance, but, in some of the developing nations and in many areas of Asia, dogs are not held in the same esteem. In some areas of the world, dogs are used as guards or beasts of burden or even for food, whereas, in the United States and Europe, dogs are protected and admired. In ancient Egypt during the days of the pharaohs, dogs were considered to be sacred.

Boxer. © R.T. Willbie/Animal Photography

Characteristics of loyalty, friendship, protectiveness, and affection have earned dogs an important position in Western society, and in the United States and Europe the care and feeding of dogs has become a multibillion-dollar business.

Dogs have played an important role in the history of human civilization and were among the first domesticated animals. They were important in hunter-gatherer societies as hunting allies and bodyguards against predators. When livestock were domesticated about 7,000 to 9,000 years ago, dogs served as herders and guardians of sheep, goats, and cattle.

German shepherd (Alsatian). © Sally Anne Thompson/Animal Photography

Although many still serve in these capacities, dogs are increasingly used for social purposes and companionship. Today, dogs are employed as guides for the blind and disabled or for police work. Dogs are even used in therapy in nursing homes and hospitals to encourage patients toward recovery. Humans have bred a wide range of different dogs adapted to serve a variety of functions. This has been enhanced by improvements in veterinary care and animal husbandry.

ORIGIN AND HISTORY OF DOGS

The modern dog is descended from the wolf (*Canis lupus*) and is classified as a wolf subspecies, *C. lupus familiaris*. The dog has evolved from the gray wolf into more than 400 distinct breeds. Human beings have played a major role in creating dogs that fulfill distinct societal needs. Through the most rudimentary form of genetic engineering, dogs were bred to accentuate instincts that were evident from their earliest encounters with humans. Although details about the evolution of dogs are uncertain, the first dogs were hunters with keen senses of sight and smell. Humans developed these instincts and created new breeds as need or desire arose.

ANCESTRY

Paleontologists and archaeologists have determined that about 60 million years ago a small mammal, rather like a weasel, lived in the environs of what are now parts of Asia. It is called *Miacis*, the genus that became the ancestor of the animals known today as canids: dogs, jackals, wolves, and foxes. *Miacis* did not leave direct descendants, but doglike canids evolved from it. By about 30 to 40 million years ago *Miacis* had evolved into the first true dog—namely, *Cynodictis*. This was a medium-size animal, longer than it was tall, with a long tail and a fairly shaggy coat. Over the millennia *Cynodictis* gave rise to two branches, one in Africa and the other in Eurasia. The Eurasian branch was called *Tomarctus* and is the progenitor of wolves, dogs, and foxes. Some genetic studies suggest that wolves were domesticated as early as 16,300 years ago to serve as livestock in China.

It is believed that the early dogs dating from about 12,000 to 14,000 years ago came from a small strain of gray wolf that inhabited what is now India. Thereafter, this wolf—known as *Canis lupus pallipes*—was widely distributed throughout Europe, Asia, and North America. It is also possible that some of the dogs of today descended not from the wolf but rather from the jackal. These dogs, found in Africa, might have given rise to some of the present native African breeds.

No matter what their origins, all canids have certain common characteristics. They are mammals that bear live young. The females have mammary glands, and they suckle their offspring. The early breeds had erect ears and pointed or wedge-shaped muzzles, similar to the northern breeds common today. Most of the carnivores have similar dental structures, which is one way paleontologists have been able to identify them. They develop two sets of teeth, deciduous ("baby") teeth and permanent teeth.

Canids walk on their toes, in contrast to an animal like the bear, which is flat-footed and walks on its heels. Dogs, like most mammals, have body hair and are homeothermic—that is to say, they have an internal thermostat that permits them to maintain their body temperature at a constant level despite the outside temperature.

Fossil remains suggest that five distinct types of dogs existed by the beginning of the Bronze Age (about 4500 BCE). They were the mastiffs, wolf-type dogs, sight hounds (such as the Saluki or greyhound), pointing dogs, and herding dogs.

DOMESTICATION

It is uncertain when the first dog became a companion of humans, but it is likely that wild canids were scavengers near tribal campsites at the same time that ancient humans discovered a hunting partner in the animals that ventured close by. In ancient Egypt, dogs were thought to possess godlike characteristics. They were pampered by their own servants, outfitted with jeweled collars, and fed the choicest diet. Only royalty was permitted to own purebred dogs, and upon the death of a ruler his favourite dog was often interred with him to protect him from harm in the afterlife.

Illustrations of dogs dating from the Bronze Age have been found on walls, tombs, and scrolls throughout Europe, the Middle East, and North America. Often the

GUIDE DOGS

Also called seeing eye dogs (for The Seeing Eye, Inc., of Morristown, N.J.), guide dogs are professionally trained to guide, protect, or aid their owners. Systematic training of guide dogs originated in Germany during World War I to aid blinded veterans.

At the age of approximately one year, the guide dog is trained for three to four months to mold its behaviour to its owner's handicap. The dog learns to adjust to a harness, stop at curbs, gauge its owner's height when traveling in low or obstructed places, and disobey a command when obedience will endanger its owner. Dogs have also been trained to perform various services for persons with hearing impairments and restricted mobility. Some dogs are trained to assist persons with seizure disorders and to summon help. Although several breeds have been educated for these roles, including Doberman pinschers and German shepherds, Labrador retrievers and Labrador-golden retriever crosses are the most widely used.

dogs are depicted hunting game with their human counterparts. Statues of dogs guard the entrances to burial crypts. In many cases these dogs clearly resemble modern canines. Such relics are indelible testimony to the importance that humans have given to the dog throughout the ages.

ORIGIN OF BREEDS

Once it became evident that dogs were faster and stronger and could see and hear better than humans, those specimens exhibiting these qualities were interbred to enhance such attributes. Fleet-footed sight hounds were revered by noblemen in the Middle East, while in Europe powerful dogs such as the mastiff were developed to protect home and traveler from harm.

As society changed and agriculture—in addition to hunting—became a means of sustaining life, other breeds of dogs were developed. Herding and guarding dogs were important to farmers for protecting their flocks. At the same time, small breeds became desirable as playthings

Chihuahua, long-coat (left) and smooth-coat (right). © Sally Anne Thompson/Animal Photography

and companions for noble families. The Pekingese in China and fragile breeds such as the Chihuahua were bred to be lapdogs. The terrier breeds were developed, mainly in England, to rid granaries and barns of rodents. Pointing and retrieving breeds were selected for special tasks related to aiding the hunter to find and capture game. Many breeds are extremely ancient, while others have been developed as recently as the 1800s.

PHYSICAL TRAITS AND FUNCTIONS

Dogs come in a wide range of shapes and sizes, yet despite their surface differences they share the most basic characteristics of the canine family.

GENERAL CHARACTERISTICS

It is difficult to imagine that a large Great Dane and a tiny poodle are of the same species, but they are genetically identical with the same anatomic features. All dogs have 78 chromosomes, or 39 pairs of chromosomes (humans have 23 pairs), and one member of each pair comes from each parent. The normal temperature (rectal) of an adult dog is 100 to 102.5 °F (38 to 39 °C).

Teeth

Dogs have two sets of teeth. Twenty-eight deciduous teeth erupt by six to eight weeks of age, and by the time puppies are six to seven months old these deciduous teeth are all replaced by 42 adult teeth. The permanent teeth include incisors, which are used to nip and bite; canines, which tear and shred flesh; and premolars and molars, which shear and crush. In short, a dog's teeth serve as weapons and as tools for cutting or tearing food. The canines are the upper and lower fangs for which the dog family was named. As in most carnivores, the teeth are high-crowned

Great Dane, ears natural (left) and cropped (right). © Ron Kimball

and pointed, unlike the broad, grinding teeth of many herbivorous animals.

The teething process can be difficult for puppies. Their gums hurt and become swollen, they may lose their appetites, and they may have mild intermittent diarrhea.

Digestive System

Dogs rarely chew their food. Once the food is taken into the mouth, it is gulped or swallowed and passed through the esophagus into the stomach, where digestive enzymes begin to break it down. Most of the digestion and absorption of food takes place in the small intestines with the aid of the pancreas and the liver. The pancreas secretes enzymes needed for regulating the digestive process. As in humans, the pancreas produces insulin and glucagon, both of which are necessary for the regulation of glucose. The liver is the largest internal organ in the body. It has six lobes (whereas the human liver has only two). The liver is responsible for many essential life-preserving functions. It helps digestion by producing bile, which aids in the absorption of fat. The liver also metabolizes protein and carbohydrates, and it excretes toxins from the bloodstream. In addition, it manufactures major blood-clotting agents. Because the liver performs all these vital functions, liver disease can be a major problem in dogs.

Skeletal Structure

The skeletal frame of the dog consists of 319 bones. If a dog's tail is docked or absent at birth, there obviously are fewer bones in the skeleton. The muscles and tendons of a dog are similar to those of a human; however, a dog's upper body muscles bear half the weight of the entire body and are better developed than a human's. The weight distribution between the front and the rear of the dog are relatively equal.

Dogs are running animals, with the exception of those bred specifically for different purposes. For instance, the bulldog, with its large head and short, "bowed" legs, cannot be called a creature born to chase game. Most dogs, however, are well equipped to run or lope over long distances, provided that they are physically conditioned for such activities. The construction of the shoulder and pelvic bones and the way they articulate with the leg bones and the spine allow most breeds to trot, run, or gallop with ease. Certain breeds have distinct gaits that have been genetically selected by humans. The German shepherd dog is known for its "flying trot." The extreme extension of the front and rear legs causes the dog to appear as if it were soaring, although one foot always remains on the ground. Another unique gait is that of the greyhound.

Bulldog. © Ron Kimball

This dog was bred for great bursts of speed, and its most comfortable gait is the gallop. The spine is unusually flexible, allowing the dog to contract and extend its four legs in unison, whereby all four feet are off the ground at the same time.

Other breeds also have unique features. The Afghan hound was bred to chase game over long distances in rocky terrain. Its structure permits great flexibility through the hip joints and lower back, enabling the dog to turn quickly in a small area. The dachshund, by contrast, is long and low with short legs. This dog was bred to hunt badgers underground, and its shape allows it to enter subterranean tunnels in search of its prey.

Although most breeds no longer follow the pursuits for which they were originally bred, their instincts remain

Afghan hound. © Kent & Donna Dannen

strong, and their structure still allows them to perform their specific tasks.

Senses

Dogs have the same five senses as humans. However, some are more highly developed, and others are deficient compared with those of humans. Dogs' sense of smell is by far the most acute and is immeasurably better than that of humans. Dogs are used for such tasks as tracking missing persons, digging underground, and tracing toxic substances, such as gases, that are undetectable by humans. Dogs can detect drugs, explosives, and the scents of their owners. Not all canine noses are the same, however. Some breeds, such as the German shepherd and the bloodhound, have much more keenly developed

Dachshund. Shutterstock.com

olfactory senses than others. One would not choose a short-nosed breed, such as the pug, to engage in tracking.

Even in short-nosed breeds, however, the olfactory centre is relatively highly developed. It is arranged in folds in order to filter smells from the incoming air. Some rescue dogs are trained to follow a scent on the ground, and others are trained to scent the air. Both are able to distinguish one person from another even after a considerable passage of time. Hunting dogs—such as pointers, retrievers, and spaniels—are trained to scent birds and can distinguish one variety of bird from another.

The dog's sense of taste is poorly developed compared with that of humans. If forced to live on their own, dogs will eat almost anything without much discrimination.

Dogs possess an acute sense of hearing. Aboriginal breeds had large, erect and very mobile ears that enabled them to hear sounds from a great distance in any direction. Some modern breeds have better hearing than others, but they all can detect noises well beyond the range of the human ear. Dogs are able to register sounds of 35,000 vibrations per second (compared with 20,000 per second in humans), and they also can shut off their inner ear in order to filter out distracting sounds.

The eyesight of a dog is not as keen as its sense of smell, and it is generally thought that dogs have poor colour perception. Some breeds, such as the Saluki and the Afghan hound, were developed to chase game by sight over long distances, and these dogs can see well enough to detect any movement far on the horizon. Dogs can generally see better in poor light than humans but not as well in bright light. They have a wider field of vision than humans because their eyes are set farther toward the sides of their heads, but they are not as adept at focusing on objects at close range nor at judging distances. Dogs have

Saluki. © Kent & Donna Dannen

a third eyelid, a membrane that protects the eyeball from irritants and is sometimes visible in front of the eye.

Dogs are sensitive to touch, the fifth sense, and use this sense to communicate with one another and with their human counterparts. Learning where to touch a dog is an important part in either stimulating or relaxing it and is useful in training a puppy or bonding with an adult dog.

Coats

There are three basic types of hair: short (as on a pointer or Doberman pinscher), medium (as on an Irish setter or Siberian husky), and long (as on a chow chow or Maltese). Within these categories there are also coarse and fine types of hair. Dogs come in a wide variety of colours, but

Irish setter. © R.T. Willbie/Animal Photography

in many breeds colour selection is an important consideration, as is the colour distribution on the dog.

Most dogs shed their coats seasonally. This is a natural occurrence that depends in large measure on the amount of available daylight. In the fall as days become shorter, a dog's coat will grow thicker and longer. In the spring the dog will begin to shed its coat, and it will take longer for the coat to grow in over the summer. Temperature influences the amount of body coat a dog grows. Dogs living in warm climates all year long rarely grow hair coats as thick as those living in colder areas, although this will affect the body coat and the amount of protective undercoat more than the topcoat or the length of furnishings on the belly, ears, and tail.

Grooming is an important part of touch to a dog and can be a pleasurable and relaxing means of relating to it.

The dog's coat forms a barrier between the environment and the skin. Grooming the coat enhances the dog's beauty and well-being and gives the owner the chance to evaluate the general health of the dog.

REPRODUCTION

There is some variation in the age at which dogs reach sexual maturity. Small breeds appear to mature faster than large ones, which usually cycle later. It is not uncommon for large-breed females to come into heat for the first time at more than 1 year of age, although 8 to 9 months is the norm. Dogs are sexually mature between 6 months and 1 year but are not socially mature until they are about 2 years of age. Females first cycle anywhere from 6 to 18 months of age and approximately twice a year thereafter. The only exception is the African basenji, which cycles annually, bearing one litter a year.

Reproductive Cycle

The heat cycle of the female lasts from 18 to 21 days. The first stage is called proestrus. It begins with mild swelling of the vulva and a bloody discharge. This lasts for about 9 days, although it may vary by 2 or 3 days. During this phase the bitch (female dog) may attract males, but she is not ready to be bred and will reject all advances. The next phase is the estrus. Usually the discharge decreases and becomes lighter, almost pink, in colour. The vulva becomes very enlarged and soft, and the bitch will be receptive to the male. This stage may last 3 or 4 days or as long as 7 to 11 days. The female may be receptive a day or two past the time when she would still be fertile. In order to be sure that the breeding is taking place at the optimum time, vaginal smears and blood tests can be done by a veterinarian beginning before estrus and through the estral phase.

HEAT (ESTRUS)

Estrus (also spelled oestrus) is the period in the sexual cycle of female mammals, except the higher primates, during which they are "in heat"—i.e., ready to accept a male and to mate. One or more periods of estrus may occur during the breeding season of a species. Prior to ovulation the endometrium (uterine lining) thickens, in preparation for holding the fertilized ova. As the proliferation of uterine tissue reaches its peak, receptivity is highest—this is the estrous period. Some animals (e.g., dogs) are monestrous, having only one heat during a breeding season. Others (e.g., ground squirrels) are polyestrous: if not impregnated, they will come into heat repeatedly during the breeding season. Males can recognize a female in heat by smell; certain substances (pheromones) are secreted only at this portion of her cycle. The female's genital area may be swollen during estrus, and she may show by a variety of behavioral signals that she is ready to mate.

At about the 14th day, or whenever estrus ends, the final, or luteal, stage of the cycle begins; this stage is called diestrus. The discharge becomes redder, the vulva returns to its normal size, and the bitch will no longer accept the male for mating. When all signs of discharge and swelling are absent, the heat is complete. The diestrus stage lasts 60 to 90 days (if no pregnancy has occurred) or until the bitch gives birth. She then enters anestrus, which is the time frame between the end of the last cycle and the beginning of the next proestrus.

Canine males are always fertile from the onset of their sexual adolescence, usually after six months of age. Larger-breed males may take a few months longer to become sexually mature. Males are usually promiscuous and are willing to mate with any available female.

Males produce far more sperm than is needed to impregnate the ova that are released during estrus. Small-breed bitches usually produce small litters. Two or three puppies in a breed such as a Yorkshire terrier is considered the norm.

Yorkshire terrier. © Sally Anne Thompson/Animal Photography

Large-breed litters can have as many as 10 or 12 puppies, although the normal bitch can suckle up to 8 at a time.

Gestation and Whelping

The normal gestation period is 63 days from the time of conception. This may vary if the bitch has been bred two or three times or if the eggs are fertilized a day or two after the mating has taken place. Eggs remain fertile for about 48 hours. Sperm can live in the vaginal tract for several days. In order to determine if a bitch is pregnant, a veterinarian can manually palpate her abdomen at about 25 days after breeding. Ultrasound also can be done at that time. At about 40 days X-rays will confirm pregnancy.

Most bitches whelp (give birth) normally. However, the large-headed, short-bodied breeds and the toy breeds often must undergo cesarean sections in order to deliver live puppies.

Reproductive Capacity

Both males and females are fertile well into their advanced age. It is generally considered best for the bitch to be bred for the first time upon maturity but not before her second or third heat cycle, depending on her age at the first. Because small breeds mature more quickly, they can be bred at an earlier age than large breeds. A bitch will have less difficulty in conceiving and carrying a litter if she is bred before the age of five. As she becomes older, litter size generally decreases. After the age of seven, bitches are likely to have small litters and experience problems in delivering the puppies. Veterinarians feel that bitches generally should not be bred after that age.

Males can be bred as long as they are fertile, although with age the motility and quantity of sperm decrease.

BEHAVIOUR

The dog is a social creature. It prefers the company of people and of other dogs to living alone. It is, therefore, considered by animal behaviourists to be a pack animal. In this respect it is similar to its distant relative the wolf. As a result of millennia of selective breeding, the dog has been adapted to live with people. Seminal studies of dog behaviour conducted in the 1950s and '60s showed, however, that dogs raised without human contact at an early age retain their inherent instincts and prefer relationships with other dogs over associations with people.

The most striking similarities between the dog and the wolf are their instinctive behaviours of play, dominance and submission, scent marking, and the females' care for their young. Wolves and dogs will mate willingly, as will dogs and coyotes. There are differences, however. The wolf matures more slowly than the dog. It reaches sexual maturity at about the age of two or three, at the same time that it achieves social maturity. A male wolf will not challenge the leaders of the pack until it is both physically and behaviorally mature. The female wolf cycles annually.

TERRITORY AND RANGE

Both dogs and wolves are territorial animals. Wolf packs, because of their need to hunt game, claim large territories as their own, whereas dogs claim their territories based on the limitations of their owners. Male wolves and dogs mark their territorial boundaries by urinating and rubbing their scent on the ground or on trees to warn other animals of their presence.

When on neutral ground, that which is not considered by either dogs or wolves to be their home territory, strangers greeting each other will go through formal rituals of sniffing, marking, tail wagging, and posturing. Unless they are claiming the same prey or are engaged in courting the same female, such interactions are usually terminated by each going its own way. Females will attack strangers in neutral territory to protect their young, however.

BARKING

Both dogs and wolves have a repertoire of barks, growls, and howls that are identifiable among themselves and to humans who have studied their vocabulary. Dog owners can determine by certain sounds whether their pet is playful, warning of a stranger nearby, fearful, or hurt. One of the earliest signs that puppies are becoming social and independent creatures within the litter are the yips and barks that they make while playing with one another. Dogs, unlike wolves, will growl if cornered or fearful. Certain breeds of dogs, notably hounds, have been bred to enhance the

Basenji. © R.T. Willbie/Animal Photography

howling instinct when they are on the trail of game. Some of the northern breeds, such as the Siberian husky, howl rather than bark. At the other end of the spectrum, the basenji does not bark but rather emits a yodeling sound when it is happy.

BEHAVIORAL DEVELOPMENT

Canine behaviour is a combination of instinct and environment. Dogs are born with certain innate characteristics that are evident from birth. Puppies are born blind and deaf, totally dependent on the dam (mother) for warmth and nourishment. The dam will instinctively suckle and protect her young, often keeping other dogs and all but the most trusted people away from the whelping box. Between 10 and 14 days after birth, the eyes and ear canals open, and the puppies begin to move actively around their nest. As they grow, they become more curious and start to investigate their surroundings independently. The dam will begin to leave them alone briefly. During this phase they relate most intensely to their littermates and dam and may become unhappy at being removed from their familiar surroundings. This stage of development lasts about 20 days and is the first of four critical periods.

Beginning at three weeks of age, the most adventurous puppies will seek ways to get out of the whelping box and will start to investigate the larger world. At this age puppies are receptive to human contact, which is essential if they are to bond with people when they become adults. Dogs left alone from four weeks on will never reach their full potential as pets and will often become independent and more difficult to train than those accustomed to close human contact from an early age. At the same time, during the period between three and seven weeks, it is important that puppies socialize with their littermates and dam. This is when the dam weans her puppies, first by regurgitating some of her own food and then by not allowing her puppies to nurse as often as they would like. At about four weeks of age, puppies can be offered solid food in the form of a soft gruel.

Individual socialization of each puppy in a litter can begin at six weeks of age. This is when puppies begin to be more receptive to handling and attention.

The third critical period in a puppy's development is from 7 to 12 weeks. It has been shown in studies undertaken at various breeding kennels that this is the best age to form human-dog relationships. Attachments formed during this period will affect the attitude of the dog toward humans and toward its acceptance of direction and learning. During this period the pack instinct, which has played such an important role in the puppy's early development, can be transferred to humans. At this time environment becomes a vital part of the dog's education and training. This is when a human can most easily establish dominance over the dog, becoming the "leader of the pack." At this age a dog will accept a submissive role more readily than at any other time in its life. Learning comes most readily at this age. Puppies taught basic commands, even if they are not reinforced for several months, will remember them and respond if they are taught during this age.

The fourth critical stage in a puppy's development is between 12 and 16 weeks. At this age the puppy will declare its independence from its mother and will become increasingly daring in its forays from the familiar. Puppy training can begin during this period, and it is a time of rapid physical and mental growth. The permanent teeth begin to emerge at this time, which is often a painful and distracting process. Puppies need to chew during this period, and, if they are not provided with appropriate teething toys, they will use any available hard object, such as furniture. Puppies at this age may be less willing to cooperate or respond to new commands.

A dog's personality continues to develop during its entire maturing process and will undergo radical changes while the dog matures sexually and physically. Dogs mature sexually earlier than they do emotionally. Their personalities develop more slowly than their bodies, much like humans but unlike wolves, whose personalities and sexuality develop more harmoniously.

At about seven or eight months many puppies tend to go through a period of anxiety. They are insecure, frightened of strangers, and will appear timid. If this is not an inherited trait, it will disappear within a few months. If it is inherited, that condition will remain and may become accentuated with time.

BREED-SPECIFIC BEHAVIOUR

There are distinctive breed-typical personalities that have been developed through generations of selection for certain traits. By roughly grouping dogs according to the work they were bred to do, it is possible to determine the type of temperament a dog might have at maturity. Differences in breed personalities can be seen at an early age. Sporting dogs will generally be adventurous, following their noses wherever scents lead them, but will respond enthusiastically to calls from familiar humans. Hounds generally tend to be more aloof and independent, inclined to scout the territory on their own and follow a scent or a movement; they are not as interested in human interaction as the bird dogs are.

Working and herding dogs have more business-like dispositions. They tend to evaluate situations and set about their tasks. Collie puppies have been known to herd children, ducklings, or each other in an instinctive manifestation of their birthright. Guarding dogs tend to be protective of their territories, even at an early age. Such dogs as the Maremma or the Kuvasz, which are bred to guard flocks, are placed with the sheep from the time they are puppies in order to reinforce their basic protective instincts. Collies and Akitas are known for their strong sense of loyalty. Terriers, bred to chase and catch rodents, have a tendency to be extremely active, lively, and feisty as puppies, traits that continue into adulthood. Newfoundlands are renowned for lifesaving instincts.

Breed specificity also affects how well dogs adapt to new surroundings or to new owners. Such things cannot be taught to dogs. They are innate—part of a dog's instinctive behaviour—and are often breed-specific, although mixed breeds have been known for unique instincts as well.

Collie. Sally Anne Thompson/EB Inc.

DOGS AS PETS

The companionship between humans and dogs is not a new phenomenon. However, in modern society most dogs are owned as pets, not because of the work they were bred to do. Many breeds, such as the toy dogs, were developed precisely to be pets. All of the diverse breeds and mixed breeds have unique traits and appeal to different kinds of people.

Acquiring a dog is a major decision, because the dog becomes totally dependent on its owner for its care and welfare. This responsibility continues throughout the life of the dog. Thus, the initial decision should be based on a serious consideration of whether one's lifestyle truly lends itself to owning a dog—that is, whether a dog would be an asset rather than a liability.

THE BREEDS

There are approximately 400 separate breeds of purebred dogs worldwide. A purebred dog is considered to be one whose genealogy is traceable for three generations within the same breed. National registries, such as the American Kennel Club (AKC) in the United States, the Canadian Kennel Club, the Kennel Club of England, and the Australian National Kennel Council, maintain pedigrees and stud books on every dog in every breed registered in their respective countries. The Foxhound Kennel Stud Book, published in England in 1844, was one of the earliest registries. The AKC represents an enrollment of more than 36 million since its inception in 1884, and it registers approximately 1.25 million new dogs each year. Other countries also have systems for registering purebred dogs.

In the 1800s those interested in the sport of dogs developed a system for classifying breeds according to their functions. The British classification, established in 1873 and revised periodically by the Kennel Club of England, set the standard that other countries have followed, with some modifications. British, Canadian, and American classifications are basically the same, although some of the terminology is different. For example, Sporting dogs in the United States are Gundogs in England. Utility dogs in England are Non-Sporting dogs in the United States and Canada. Not all countries recognize every breed.

The United States recognizes seven classifications, called groups (encompassing more than 150 breeds), whereas the English and Canadians have six groups (the American system divides the Working group into two groups: Working dogs and Herding dogs).

BREED STANDARDS

Purebred dogs are distinguished from mixed-breed animals because their genetic structure allows them to reproduce themselves generation after generation.

Every breed that is registered with a national registry, such as the American Kennel Club or the Kennel Club of England, must have a "standard" for that breed. The standard is the blueprint by which a breed is evaluated. It describes the characteristics that make a particular breed unique. Standards were developed by fanciers who wanted to perpetuate a particular line or strain and who formed associations to foster certain breeds. It is the goal of most purebred-dog fanciers to breed dogs that best represent the ideal qualities for the breed as described by the standard. Standards outline requirements for physical traits and behavioral or "personality" traits.

Sporting Dogs

These are dogs that scent and either point, flush, or retrieve birds on land and in water. They are the pointers, retrievers, setters, spaniels, and others, such as the Vizsla and the Weimaraner.

German shorthaired pointer. © Sally Anne Thompson/Animal Photography

HOUNDS

These also are hunting dogs but much more various than the Sporting dogs. There are scent hounds and sight hounds. They are a diverse group, ranging from the low-slung dachshund to the fleet-footed greyhound. However, they all are dedicated to the tasks for which they were bred, whether coursing over rough terrain in search of gazelles, such as the Afghan hound or the Saluki, or going to ground after badgers, like the dachshund. Hounds such as beagles, basset hounds, harriers, foxhounds, and coonhounds run in packs, while others, such as Afghan hounds, borzois, pharaoh hounds, and Salukis, course

Bloodhound. © Sally Anne Thompson/Animal Photography

alone. The Hound group also includes the Petit Basset Griffon Vendéen, the otterhound, the Rhodesian ridgeback, which was bred to hunt lions in Africa, and the bloodhound, best known for its remarkable ability to track. The Irish wolfhound, Scottish deerhound, basenji, whippet, and Norwegian elkhound are also in this group. In Canada, drevers belong to the Hound group as well, and in England the Grand Basset Griffon Vendéen is included.

Terriers

The Terrier group consists of both big and small dogs, but members of this group more than any other share a common ancestry and similar behavioral traits. Terriers were bred to rid barns and stables of vermin, to dig out unwanted burrowing rodents, and to make themselves generally useful around the stable. Terriers were used in the "poor man's recreation" of rat killing, especially in England where most of these breeds originated. Upper classes used terriers in foxhunting. They also were bred to fight each other in pits—hence the name pit bulls. During the late 1900s, dogfighting was outlawed in most states and countries of the Western world, and these dogs were thereafter bred for a friendly temperament rather than for aggressiveness.

Terriers, because they had to fit in burrows and dig underground, were bred to stay relatively small, although large breeds are not uncommon. Their coats are usually rough and wiry for protection and require minimum maintenance. Unlike hounds or sporting dogs, which only found or chased their quarry, terriers were often required to make the actual kill as well, giving them a more pugnacious temperament than their size might suggest. They are usually lean with long heads, square jaws, and deep-set eyes. However, as with most breeds, form follows function:

terriers that work underground have shorter legs, while terriers bred to work aboveground have squarer proportions. All terriers are active and vocal, naturally inclined to chase and confront.

The small terriers, which were often carried on horseback during foxhunts, were bred to be put to the ground. These dogs have very specific origins. In general, their names reflect the locale where the breed first took shape under the guidance of a small group of dedicated breeders. They are the Australian, Bedlington, border, cairn, Dandie Dinmont, Lakeland, Manchester, miniature schnauzer (of German origin), Norwich, Norfolk, Scottish, Sealyham, Skye, Welsh, and West Highland white. The larger terriers include the Airedale, Irish, Kerry blue, and soft-coated wheaten. In Canada, Lhasa apsos are part of this group. Britain claims the Parson

Black miniature schnauzer. Shutterstock.com

Jack Russell and the Glen of Imaal terriers, both of which are found in the United States but are not registerable with the AKC.

WORKING DOGS

This group of dogs was bred to serve humans in very practical and specific ways. They are the dogs most often associated with guarding, leading, guiding, protecting, pulling, or saving lives. Working dogs range in size from medium to large, but all are robust with sturdy and muscular builds. Working dogs are characterized by strength and alertness, intelligence, and loyalty.

Doberman pinscher. © Kent & Donna Dannen

Among the breeds most often associated with guarding home, person, or property are the Akita, boxer, bullmastiff, Doberman pinscher, giant schnauzer, Great Dane, mastiff, Rottweiler, and standard schnauzer. Dogs bred to guard livestock are the Great Pyrenees, komondor, and Kuvasz. In England, Pyrenean mountain dogs are recognized in this group, as are all the herding dogs, and, in Canada, Eskimo dogs are included. Also in the Working group are those dogs bred to pull, haul, and rescue. These include the Alaskan Malamute and Siberian husky, the Samoyed, the Bernese mountain dog, the Portuguese water dog, the Newfoundland, and the St. Bernard. Poodles of the three varieties (standard, miniature, and toy) are part of this group in England, as are several other breeds found in the Non-Sporting group in the United States.

Herding Dogs

The Herding breeds are livestock-oriented, although they are versatile in protecting and serving humans in other ways. Herding breeds are intelligent and lively, making fine family pets or obedience competitors. Dogs were first used to assist sheepherders in the 1570s, but other varieties were bred for different herding tasks. Herding breeds are quick and agile, able to work on any terrain, and well-suited for short bursts of high speed. These dogs, even the compact breeds, are strong and muscular, possessing proud carriage of head and neck. Herding dogs perceive even the slightest hand signals and whistle commands to move a flock or seek out strays.

Some Herding breeds drive the flock by barking, circling, and nipping at the heels, while others simply confront the flock with a silent stare, which also proves effective.

Australian shepherd. © Kent & Donna Dannen

Herding dogs serve other functions. These breeds are excellent guards, used in the military and law enforcement, or for personal protection. Herding dogs are among those with the closest relationship to humans.

Toys

The Toy group is composed of those canines that were bred specifically to be companion animals. They were developed to be small, portable, and good-natured, the sort of dog that ladies of the court could carry with them. These dogs were largely pampered and treasured by aristocracy around the world. Several of these breeds come from ancient lineage. The Pekingese and the Japanese

Pug. © Kent & Donna Dannen

Chin were owned by royalty. No one else was permitted to own one of these breeds. They were carefully bred and nurtured, and until the mid-20th century they were not allowed to be exported out of their countries of origin. In England the cavalier King Charles spaniel, a bred-down version of a sporting spaniel, was the favourite pet of many royal families. Cavaliers, while popular in the United States, are not registered with the AKC, but their close cousins, the English toy spaniels are. Toy poodles also belong to this group, as does the pug.

The miniature pinscher resembles the Doberman pinscher but in fact is of quite different legacy. This perky little dog has a particularly distinctive gait, found in no other breed. Its standard calls for a hackney gait, such as that found in carriage horses. Other members of the Toy group are equally individual in their looks and personalities, making this the most diverse group. They make ideal apartment or small-house pets and are found ranging from hairless (the Chinese crested) to the profusely coated Pekingese or Shih tzu. In general, however, Toy breeds are alert and vigorous dogs. They are fine-boned and well-balanced, often considered graceful animals.

NON-SPORTING DOGS

The Non-Sporting group is a catchall category for those breeds that do not strictly fit into any other group. (Arguments could be made for assigning some of these breeds to other groups. The Dalmatian, for instance, could be a Working dog, as it is in England.) This group includes the appealing bichon frise, the bulldog, the poodles

Dalmatian. © Ron Kimball

(standard and miniature), and the Chinese shar-pei. All have unique histories, many quite ancient. Other Asian representatives are the Tibetan spaniel and the Tibetan terrier—neither of which are true spaniels or terriers—the chow chow, and the Lhasa apso. Non-Sporting is also the category for the Finnish spitz, the Keeshond, the French bulldog, and the schipperke. All the Non-Sporting breeds are of small to medium build with sturdy and balanced frames, often squarelike. The chow chow, French bulldog, and the Dalmatian are among the more muscular breeds in this group. In general, Non-Sporting dogs are alert and lively.

There is no comparable classification in Britain, although all these breeds, except for the Boston terrier, are found in other groups. The Boston terrier (not a true terrier although it once contained terrier blood) is one of the few native American dogs. (Others include the Alaskan Malamute, the American foxhound, American Staffordshire terrier, American water spaniel, the Chesapeake Bay retriever, and the American cocker spaniel, all found in other groups.)

DOMESTIC CATS

The familiar house cat (*Felis catus*) is a domesticated member of the family Felidae, order Carnivora. Like all felines, domestic cats, the smallest members of the family, are characterized by supple, low-slung bodies, finely molded heads, long tails that aid in balance, and specialized teeth and claws that adapt them admirably to a life of active hunting. Domestic cats possess other features of their wild relatives in being basically carnivorous, remarkably agile and powerful, and finely coordinated in movement.

Himalayan, chocolate point. © Chanan Photography

ORIGIN AND HISTORY OF CATS

The "cat pattern," established very early in the evolution of modern mammals, was a successful one: early cats were already typical in form at a time when the ancestors of most other modern mammalian types were scarcely recognizable. They first appeared in the early Pliocene Epoch (5.3 to 3.6 million years ago), and they have continued with remarkably little change into modern times.

DOMESTICATION

Although its origin is hidden in antiquity, the domestic cat has a history that dates nearly 3,500 years to ancient Egypt. There are no authentic records of domestication earlier than 1500 BCE, but it may have taken place sooner. Although the cat was proclaimed a sacred animal in the 5th

Abyssinian, red, or sorrel. © Chanan Photography

and 6th dynasties (c. 2465 to c. 2150 BCE), it had not neces-
sarily been domesticated at that time. It is probable that
the Egyptians domesticated the cat because they realized
its value in protecting granaries from rodents. Their affection and respect for this predator led to the development
of religious cat cults and temple worship of cats.

Cats have long been known to other cultures. Wall
tiles in Crete dating from 1600 BCE depict hunting
cats. Evidence from art and literature indicates that
the domestic cat was present in Greece from the 5th
century BCE and in China from 500 BCE. In India cats
were mentioned in Sanskrit writings around 100 BCE,
while the Arabs and the Japanese were not introduced
to the cat until about 600 CE. The earliest record of

Manx, red mackerel tabby and white. © Marc Henrie

cats in Britain dates to about 936 CE, when Hywel Dda, prince of south-central Wales, enacted laws for their protection.

Even though all cats are similar in appearance, it is difficult to trace the ancestry of individual breeds. Since tabbylike markings appear in the drawings and mummies of ancient Egyptian cats, present-day tabbies may be descendants of the sacred cats of Egypt. The Abyssinian also resembles pictures and statues of Egyptian cats. The Persian, whose colouring is often the same as that of mixed breeds (although the length of hair and the body conformation are distinctive), was probably crossed at various times with other breeds; the tailless Manx cat, like the hairless Sphynx cat and curly-coated Devon rex, is a mutation. The ancestry of Persian and Siamese cats may well be distinct from other domestic breeds, representing a domestication of an Asian wild cat (the ancestor of the Egyptian cat is believed to have come from Africa). In fact, nothing is known of the ancestry of the Siamese types, and there is no living species of Asian cat that would serve as ancestor.

Sphynx. © Chanan Photography

The cat has long played a role in religion and witchcraft. In the Bible, "cat" is mentioned only in the apocryphal Letter of Jeremiah. The cat figured prominently in the religions of Egypt, the Norse countries, and various parts of Asia. The Egyptians had a cat-headed goddess named Bast. Thousands of cat mummies have been discovered in Egypt, and there were even mouse mummies, presumably to provide food for the cats. Often the cat has been associated with sorcery and witchcraft, and the superstitions regarding cats are innumerable. Throughout the ages, cats have been more cruelly mistreated than perhaps any other animal. Black cats in particular have long been regarded as having occult powers and as being the familiars of witches.

The cat is a well-known figure in nursery rhymes, stories, and proverbs. The English legend of Dick Whittington and his cat is a particular favourite. The writers Théophile Gautier and Charles Baudelaire paid it homage, and in the 20th century Rudyard Kipling, Colette, and T.S. Eliot wrote of cats.

GENERAL FEATURES AND SPECIAL ADAPTATIONS

The average weight of the household cat varies from 2.5 to 4.5 kg (6 to 10 pounds), although among nonpedigreed cats weights of up to 12.5 kg (28 pounds) are not uncommon. Average lengths are 70 cm (28 inches) for males and 50 cm (20 inches) for females. In keeping with a carnivorous habit, the cat has a simple gut; the small intestine is only about three times the length of the body.

The skin of the cat, composed of dermis and epidermis, regenerates and fights off infection quickly. Tiny erector muscles, attached to hair follicles, enable the cat to bristle all over. Thus, although the cat is a relatively small animal, it can frighten enemies by arching its back, bristling, and hissing.

COORDINATION AND MUSCULATURE

Cats are among the most highly specialized of the flesh-eating mammals. Their brains are large and well developed. Cats are digitigrade; that is, they walk on their toes. Unlike the dog and horse, the cat walks or runs by moving first the front and back legs on one side, then the front and back legs on the other side; only the camel and the giraffe move in a similar way. The cat's body has great elasticity. Because the vertebrae of the spinal column are held together by muscles rather than by ligaments, as in humans, the cat can elongate or contract its back, curve it upward, or oscillate it along the vertebral line. The construction of the shoulder joints permits the cat to turn its foreleg in almost any direction. Cats are powerfully built animals and are so well coordinated that they almost invariably land on their feet if they fall or are dropped.

TEETH

The cat's teeth are adapted to three functions: stabbing (canines), anchoring (canines), and cutting (molars). Cats have no flat-crowned crushing teeth and therefore cannot chew their food; instead, they cut it up. Except for the canines and molars, the cat's teeth are more or less nonfunctional; most of the cheek teeth do not even meet when the mouth is closed. The dental formula in all cats, for either side of both upper and lower jaws, is incisors 3/3, canines 1/1, premolars 3/2, and molars 1/1. The total number of teeth is 16 in the upper jaw and 14 in the lower.

Primary, or milk, teeth number 24; these are replaced by the permanent teeth at about five months. Each half of the jaw is hinged to the skull by a transverse roller that fits tightly into a trough on the underside of the skull, making grinding movements impossible even if the cat had teeth suitable for grinding.

CLAWS

There is a remarkable mechanism for retracting the cat's claws when they are not in use. The claw is retracted or extended by pivoting the end bone of the toe, which bears the claw, over the tip of the next bone. The action that unsheathes the claws also spreads the toes widely, making the foot more than twice as broad as it normally is and converting it into a truly formidable weapon. This claw-sheathing mechanism is present in all species of the cat family except the cheetah. Although there are no nerve endings in the nail itself, blood capillaries are present in the inner part.

THE DOMESTIC SHORTHAIR

The domestic shorthair is a breed of domestic cat often referred to

as the common alley cat. However, it is a good show animal, has been purebred and pedigreed, and has been carefully bred to conform to a set standard of appearance. The domestic shorthair is required by show standards to be a sturdily built cat with strong-boned legs and a round head

Domestic shorthair cat. John Gajda/EB Inc.

with round eyes and ears that are rounded at the tips. The coat must be short and may be any of the colours recognized for the longhair, or Persian. Some colours, such as blue cream, are infrequently found in shorthairs; others, such as the tabby colours (silver, brown, blue, and red), are commoner. In Britain, the shorthair is called the British shorthair to distinguish it from other breeds classified as foreign shorthairs.

British Shorthair, blue, cream, and white dilute calico. © Chanan Photography

Although the alley cat may resemble a pedigreed shorthair, it is not a purebred animal; rather, it is a combination of breeds and may differ considerably in build and coat from the purebred shorthair.

SENSES

Cats are generally nocturnal in habit. The retina of the cat's eye is made extra sensitive to light by a layer of guanine, which causes the eye to shine at night in a strong light. The eyes themselves, large with pupils that expand or contract to mere slits according to the density of light, do not distinguish colours clearly. Cats have a third eyelid, or nictitating membrane, commonly called the haw. Its appearance is used frequently as an indicator of the cat's general state of health.

The cat's sense of smell, particularly well developed in the adult, is crucial to its evaluation of food, so that a cat whose nasal passages become clogged as a result of illness may appear to lose its appetite completely. Cats can distinguish the odour of nitrogenous substances (e.g., fish) especially keenly.

The sense of touch is acute in cats. The eyebrows, whiskers, hairs of the cheek, and fine tufts of hair on the ears are all extremely sensitive to vibratory stimulation. The functions of the whiskers (vibrissae) are only partially understood; however, it is known that, if they are cut off, the cat is temporarily incapacitated. The toes and paws, as well as the tip of the nose, are also very sensitive to touch.

Cats also have an acute sense of hearing. Their ears contain 32 muscles (compared with 6 in humans and 12 in dogs); as a result, they can turn them many times more quickly in the direction of a sound than can a dog. The ears of cats, although receptive to ultrasonic frequencies up to 25,000 vibrations per second, are slightly inferior to those of dogs, which register 35,000 vibrations per second.

BEHAVIOUR

The cat has a subtle repertoire of facial expressions, vocal sounds, and tail and body postures that express its emotional state and intentions. These various signals serve to increase, decrease, or maintain social distance. One distinctive social behaviour involves rubbing the side of the head, lips, chin, or tail against the owner and against furniture. These regions of the cat's body contain scent glands that seem to play a role in establishing a familiar odour in the cat's environment.

The tongue of all cats, which has a patch of sharp, backward-directed spines near the tip, has the appearance and feel of a coarse file; the spines help the cat to lap up liquids and also to groom itself. The disposition to cleanliness is well established in cats, and they groom themselves at length, especially after meals.

While lions and other big cats roar, domestic cats and other *Felis* species purr. Purring has been described as a low, continuous, rattling hum and often is interpreted as an expression of pleasure or contentment. Purring also occurs in cats that are injured and in pain, however, so that this vocalization can be seen as the cat's "mantra"—that is, as a relaxing, self-comforting sound and a friendly mood-conveying signal.

THE LONGHAIR

Persian, cream and white bicolour. © Chanan Photography

The longhair is a breed of domestic cat noted for its long, soft, flowing coat. Long-haired cats were originally known as Persians, or Angoras. These names were later discarded in favour of the name longhair, although the cats are still commonly called Persians in the United States. The longhair, a medium-sized or large cat with a cobby (stocky), short-legged body, has a broad, round head, a snub nose, and a short, heavily haired tail. The large, round eyes may be blue, orange, golden, green, or copper-coloured, depending on the colour of the cat. The soft, finely textured coat forms a heavy ruff about the neck.

The longhair is bred in a number of colour varieties. The solid, or self, colours are white, black, blue, red, and cream. Patterned coats include shaded silver and black (smoke); silver, brown, blue, or red with darker markings (tabby); white finely ticked with black (chinchilla); cream, red, and black (tortoiseshell); calico, or tortoiseshell and white; blue-gray and cream intermingled (blue cream); and bicoloured. The colours of tortoiseshells, calicos, and blue creams are genetically linked with the sex of the cat. Almost all are females, and most of the few males are sterile. Blue-eyed white cats may be deaf.

Longhairs with Siamese markings (i.e., pale body and dark face, ears, legs, and tail) are Himalayans, or colourpoints. Similarly marked longhairs with white paws are called Birmans. Peke-faced longhairs have short, pushed-in, Pekingese-like faces.

Longhair cats, although generally considered more languorous than short-haired cats, are, like shorthairs, noted for playfulness, affection, and the ability to defend themselves if necessary.

BEHAVIORAL PROBLEMS

Under conditions of domestication, the cat is subject to a variety of factors that result in behaviour indicative of emotional distress and difficulty in adapting to the home environment. Some behaviours are not abnormal but are difficult for owners to accept.

The most common behaviour problem in companion cats is that they sometimes urinate and defecate outside the litter box in the house. Organic causes include feline urologic syndrome (urinary bladder inflammation and calculi, or stones, in the urinary tract), blocked or impacted anal glands, and constipation. Emotional causes include the addition of a new family member—another cat, a child, or a spouse. Such changes may make the cat feel insecure, so that it deposits urine and feces around the house, possibly as territorial marks for security. Cats are creatures of habit, and any change in the family structure or in daily routines—resulting, for example, from a move or even from rearranging furniture—can be stressful.

Another common behaviour problem in cats is their natural desire to rake objects such as drapes and furniture with their claws. Surgical removal of the front claws to prevent property damage is normally repugnant to cat lovers. Cats can be trained to use carpeted scratching posts in the house to satisfy this behavioral need, which may be a combination of claw cleaning and sharpening and of territorial marking.

Many cats engage in social licking and in the grooming of their feline and human companions, which is a natural display of affection and dependence. Some also engage in nursing behaviour, sucking on people's fingers and earlobes, on their own paws and tails, and on blankets and woolen clothing. Nursing may be a cat's way of regressing and relaxing into kittenish behaviour. It is often more intense in cats weaned too early or in those malnourished in kittenhood. For various emotional reasons some cats may groom themselves to the point of self-mutilation or become compulsive wool suckers and eaters.

Pica—a hunger for nonnutritive substances—may be a symptom of the need for more roughage in the diet or of feline leukemia or other health problems. As with the dog, excessive eating and drinking is frequently associated with endocrine diseases such as diabetes and thyroid dysfunction. Cats often vomit soon after eating, which is most often caused by the accumulation of fur balls in the stomach, although a food allergy, feline leukemia, or other organic cause may be involved.

Active and healthy cats often race through the house as though they were crazed. These "evening crazies" (which can also erupt early in the morning) result from the cat's ancient rhythm of actively hunting around dawn and dusk. In the domestic environment, this normal, instinctive behaviour often still occurs, to the consternation of some owners who fear that their cat may have rabies, a brain tumour, or an unstable personality.

Changes in animals' behaviour should not, therefore, be dismissed as psychological (or as simple disobedience, as when a cat suddenly becomes unhousebroken, for example), since there may be an underlying physical cause.

Nevertheless, abnormal behaviour in animals often does have a nonphysical, psychological, or emotional origin, which should always be considered in the diagnosis and treatment of the ailments of companion animals.

OTHER TRAITS

The cat's sleep patterns are different from those of dogs and humans. Dogs and humans have long periods of REM (rapid eye movement) sleep, the stage that is associated with dreaming. In contrast, the cat rarely lapses into REM sleep. Instead, it has a lighter, episodic sleep pattern that enables it to rest but to be instantly alert. When sick, cats have a tendency to withdraw and become inactive, which helps them conserve energy. A sick cat may seem lifeless but recover after a few days of withdrawal, which is one reason cats are said to have nine lives. (A sick cat should always be taken to a veterinarian, however; it is negligent simply to let nature take its course.)

Cats are known to have traveled hundreds of miles to find their owners in new homes to which they themselves have never been. Dogs have also performed such feats of so-called psi (psychic) trailing. Scientists have not been able to find a physiological or psychological explanation for this uncanny ability.

CATS AS PETS

The popularity of the cat, especially of pedigreed breeds, has continued to grow. The cat's independent personality, grace, cleanliness, and subtle displays of affection have wide appeal. Typically, cats are creatures of habit; they are inquisitive, but not adventurous, and are easily upset by sudden changes of routine. The ideal household cat has been separated from its mother between the ages of two

Cats raised together from kittenhood tend to get along well and can keep each other company. Hope Lourie Kilcoyne

and four months, raised in a clean home, kept away from unhealthy animals, and inoculated against common infectious cat diseases. Although cats often enjoy the company of other cats, especially when raised together from kittenhood, introducing a strange cat to other cats in the home can cause stress, aggression, and other behaviour problems. Cats are generally less sociable than dogs, who more readily accept a new pack member.

A good disposition and good health are important criteria for choosing a cat. Disposition varies only slightly between male and female cats. There are, however, distinct differences in disposition among the various pedigreed varieties; the Siamese, for example, is vocal and demanding, while the Persian is quiet and fastidious. The mixed breed is a heterogeneous breed of unknown lineage, and therefore its disposition is difficult to assess. By chance, the mixed breed may prove a happier and healthier pet than a pedigreed one. On the other hand, the behaviour and vigour of the direct ancestors of pedigreed cats are indicative of the characteristics the offspring will possess as adults. But, as with the propagation of purebred dogs, the proliferation of pedigreed cats has resulted in an increase in inherited diseases, a major reason many people prefer mongrels or mixed breeds.

NUTRITION

Domestic cats should have a diet similar to that of their wild relatives. They are adapted by nature to be flesh eaters, as is shown by their alimentary tract and their dentition. The cat uses its canines to catch and kill prey, the molars to cut it up. Lack of flat-surfaced teeth prevents it from chewing or gnawing. The cat has a short intestine, and its stomach secretes digestive juices that act primarily on meat. Cats, however, like all meat-eating animals, ingest grass and other plants occasionally, and small quantities of vegetables may serve as both a laxative and a hair ball remover.

As cats are the strictest of all carnivorous mammals, they thrive on meat, but an all-meat diet is unbalanced and will lead to various nutritional deficiency diseases. Cats derive nutrients, including moisture, from their entire prey—hence the low thirst drive of most cats. Commercial dry pet foods, lacking moisture and overloaded with starches, are convenient for the owner but can contribute to many of the most common feline ailments—including obesity, urinary tract diseases, and diabetes mellitus. The system of a strictly carnivorous animal is not equipped to handle a high dietary proportion of carbohydrates nor to digest grain matter. It is therefore prudent to examine the ingredient list on commercial cat foods, including "prescription" foods, which often contain species-inappropriate ingredients and have no logical place in a cat's diet. In addition, seafood is not recommended; many cats are allergic to it, and it may be contaminated with hazardous chemicals.

Getting as close to the natural carnivorous diet as possible by feeding a low-carbohydrate, meat-based diet can eliminate many of the most common ailments and diseases, which are not only painful for cats but also quite costly. Feline experts advise against ever feeding cats all-dry manufactured foods, because cats often grow to prefer those to the degree that they refuse other, healthier foods.

REPRODUCTION

Domestic cats reach reproductive age between 7 and 12 months. A breeding female (called a queen) can be in heat, or estrus, as many as five times a year. During these periods, which last about five days, the cat "calls," or caterwauls, intermittently. The gestation period for cats averages 63 to 65 days, and birth usually lasts about two hours. The birth is often called kittening, and the kittens are called a litter. The average litter numbers four; however, the Abyssinian usually has fewer, the Siamese more.

Each kitten is born in a separate amniotic sac that is generally broken open at the moment of birth. If it is not, the mother breaks it. She also severs the umbilical cord and eats the placenta (which in many cases stimulates lactation). The kittens are born blind, deaf, and helpless, as are many other carnivores; their senses begin to function 10 or 12 days after birth. Soon after birth the mother licks her kittens; this action cleans them and helps stimulate their circulation. Kittens at birth lack distinctive colouring, and many do not acquire their characteristic markings and colour for weeks. For example, Siamese kittens are white at birth, while blue Persians have tabby markings and black Persians are brown.

Unlike wild cats that breed once a year, the domestic cat is capable of bearing up to three litters every year. Traditionally, regulation of the cat population was accomplished by the selective killing of the newborn. In modern times, however, sterilization—by means of relatively safe and simple operations known as spaying, neutering, or altering—has become common in affluent societies. Neutering is also viewed as an adaptive measure for indoor life.

Castration of the male, ideally around six or seven months of age, helps control the adult male's tendency to "spray"—to mark objects in and around the house with his own urine. Spaying the female may help reduce the incidence of breast cancer in addition to eliminating uterine diseases and unwanted litters.

Neutered cats live longer than nonneutered ones, partly because they have less desire to roam. The average life expectancy for the domestic cat is 10 to 15 years; the oldest cat on record attained the age of 34 years.

DISEASES AND PARASITES

For many years cat treatments were simply extensions of those given dogs. Now, however, cat disorders of the skin, the eyes, the ears, the various systems (circulatory, respiratory, urinary, digestive, nervous, skeletal), and the blood, as well as contagious cat diseases and external and internal parasites, are studied, so that appropriate preventions and treatments can be developed.

Many cats die because their ailments become serious before their general conditions change sufficiently to reveal symptoms of illness. On the other hand, many symptoms used in diagnosing cat ailments are not definitive for given disorders. For example, signs of illness include general symptoms such as a dull coat, lack of appetite, and listlessness. Diarrhea may be a result of serious illness or simply reflect a change in diet. Tearing of the eyes, especially when accompanied by sneezing, may indicate conjunctivitis or a cold. Since, however, sneezing is the cat's only mechanism for blowing its nose, not all sneezing indicates illness. Open sores, usually at the base of the ear, around the mouth, or on the toes, can point to an ear mite or a ringworm infection or to a fight with another animal.

Cats are attacked by several kinds of external and internal parasites. External parasites are most generally found in kittens, although they can occur in adults. The most frequent parasites are fleas, but lice, ticks, and ear mites also occur. Internal parasites include roundworms, tapeworms, and protozoan coccidia. Modern veterinary medicine has made all of these easy to control.

Panleucopenia, often called feline distemper, is the best-known viral disease in cats. Highly contagious, with a high mortality rate, it is seen most often in young cats. Vaccines are effective protective measures. Rabies is less of a problem with cats than with dogs, but all free-roaming cats should be vaccinated. Vaccines have also been developed for other feline diseases, including feline leukemia, pneumonitis (chlamydiosis), viral rhinotracheitis (cat influenza), and calicivirus infections.

Cats permitted to wander outdoors are exposed to a variety of hazards, including accidents, attacks from other animals, poisoning, fleas and other parasites, and contagious diseases such as feline acquired immune deficiency syndrome (AIDS). Cats that kill and eat rodents and other small animals can become infected with the parasitic protozoan *Toxoplasma gondii,* which can be transmitted to humans and causes the disease toxoplasmosis.

GENETICS

Cats have never been bred for economic purposes; their matings are extremely difficult to control unless the animals are completely confined. There has been relatively little scientific breeding of cats, and the facts of inheritance in these animals are not well known.

Cats are genetically far less plastic than dogs and therefore have not offered the same opportunities to breeders. The size differences between breeds in the domestic dog have no parallel in the domestic cat, nor has anything even remotely approaching the wide range of head shapes and body proportions in different breeds of dogs ever appeared in the cats. In cats the physical differences between one breed and another are largely differences in colour and texture of the coat.

COLOUR

The most common coat colours are blotched tabby, black, and orange. The latter term refers to the gene responsible for the expression of creams, yellows, gingers, and reds ("yellow" and "red" can also refer to this group of colours). Solid white is dominant to all other colours. Tortoiseshell, a piebald pattern that results from crossing a black, tabby, or other nonorange colour with a colour from the orange group, is a sex-linked trait. The orange gene is carried on the X chromosome; male tortoiseshells have one extra X chromosome, resulting in an abnormal XXY chromosomal pattern. Hence, male tortoiseshells are born only rarely and are usually sterile. Similarly, tortoiseshell-and-white cats (in North America sometimes called calicoes) are almost always female.

Siamese dilution, the typical coloration of Siamese cats, has been described as a case of imperfect albinism and has been compared to the Himalayan pattern in rabbits, but its heredity is not well understood. There are also dilutions of the other ordinary colours: blue is dilute black and cream is dilute yellow. White spotting also occurs and is dominant to uniform colour.

OTHER CHARACTERS

The long-haired coat of the Persian appears to be a simple unit character. It is recessive to short hair. Eye colour is known to be inherited, but its mode of inheritance is not thoroughly understood. Blue eye colour seems to be associated with dilution in coat colour; blue-eyed white cats are usually deaf, a fact commented on by Charles Darwin. Asymmetry of eye colour is inherited. Polydactylism, the presence of extra toes, is inherited and behaves as a dominant to the normal condition. It seems to be due to a single gene. The extra toes occur on the inner, or thumb, side of the foot.

BREEDS

The number of recognized show breeds that have defined, inherited characteristics has increased dramatically since the late 1950s as cats have become more popular as home companions. The 30 to 40 distinctive breeds can be grouped into two general categories: the long-haired Persian and the domestic shorthair. Both of these breeds occur in various subcategories based on their coat colour, such as white, cream, chinchilla (or silver), smoke, tortoiseshell, and tabby (red, blue, and so on). Other distinctive and popular breeds include the Siamese (with

Bengal. © Chanan Photography

seal point, blue point, chocolate point, and lilac point colour variations), the long-haired Himalayan, which resembles the Siamese in coloration, and the Abyssinian, Burmese, Manx, rex, and Russian blue.

CONCLUSION

A review of the anatomy of every species of Carnivora seems to confirm that these animals are made for hunting and killing. Relatively large brains give them the intelligence to match wits with their swift and careful prey. Forward-directed eyes, large ears, and long muzzles allow them to see, hear, and smell other animals before they are detected themselves. Long legs and reduced (or even absent) collarbones give many carnivores extra speed and suppleness for chasing and pouncing. Strong claws (sometimes retractable, as in the cats) are made for digging after prey or pulling it down. Finally, and perhaps most obviously, teeth that include long canines for puncturing and holding, incisors for nipping and tearing, and premolars for shearing are clearly specialized for dispatching living prey and tearing flesh.

For such reasons carnivores are animals to be feared. Frequently, their tendency to raid domestic livestock has led to their being hunted relentlessly—as has happened to wolves, foxes, hyenas, and pumas—and nothing is more alarming than a report of a bear or tiger that, for one reason or another, has become a "man eater." Yet the hunting qualities of carnivores also have been prized by humans, most notably in domestic dogs but also in cheetahs and in smaller carnivores such as ferrets, mongooses, and even skunks. The relationship between human and dog—*Homo sapiens* and *Canis lupus familiaris*—in particular makes for one of the most interesting stories in animal evolution and behaviour. In addition, the furs of some carnivores, from the minks and other members of the weasel family to spotted cats such as the ocelot, have fetched high prices for their beauty and luxuriousness.

Clearly the relationship between carnivores and people is not strictly one of predator and prey. In many cases carnivores have been trapped, made captive, domesticated, harvested, or hunted to the point of extinction. For some large carnivores, such as bears and the big cats, human beings are their only natural enemies, and virtually all carnivores have been put under pressure as humans have altered or reduced their native habitats. As more becomes known about the role of carnivores in the environment—especially the beneficial role played by their hunting in maintaining the balance of animal populations—it may become necessary that human beings reappraise their traditional attitudes toward these very important animals.

*A*PPENDICES

APPENDIX I

DOG BREEDS AND THEIR PLACES OF ORIGIN		
CONTINENT	**COUNTRY**	**BREED**
North America	Canada	Labrador retriever, Eskimo dog, Nova Scotia duck tolling retriever, Newfoundland
	Cuba	Havanese
	Mexico	Chihuahua, Mexican hairless
	United States	Alaskan Malamute, American foxhound, American Staffordshire terrier, American water spaniel, Australian shepherd, Boston terrier, Chesapeake Bay retriever, coonhound
South America	Peru	Inca hairless dog, Peruvian Inca orchid
Europe	Belgium	Belgian Malinois, Belgian sheepdog, Belgian Tervuren, bouvier de Flandres, Brussels griffon, schipperke
	Croatia	Dalmatian
	England	Airedale terrier, beagle, Bedlington terrier, bull terrier, bulldog (English), bullmastiff, Cavalier King Charles spaniel, cocker spaniel, curly-coated retriever, English foxhound, English setter, English springer spaniel, English toy spaniel, field spaniel,

CONTINENT	COUNTRY	BREED
Europe		flat-coated retriever, fox terrier, harrier, Jack Russell terrier, Lakeland terrier, Manchester terrier, mastiff, Norfolk terrier, Norwich terrier, Old English sheepdog, otterhound, pointer, springer spaniel, Staffordshire bull terrier, Sussex spaniel, whippet, Yorkshire terrier
	Great Britain	collie, bearded collie, border collie, border terrier, Dandie Dinmont terrier
	Finland	Finnish spitz, Karelian bear dog
	France	basset hound, briard, Britanny, Clumber spaniel, French bulldog, Great Pyrenees, Löwchen
	Germany	affenpinscher, boxer, dachshund, Doberman pinscher, German shepherd dog, German shorthaired pointer, German wirehaired pointer, Great Dane, miniature pinscher, poodle, Rottweiler, schnauzer, Weimaraner
	Iceland	Iceland dog
	Ireland	Irish setter, Irish red and white setter, Irish water spaniel, Irish wolfhound, Irish terrier, Kerry blue terrier, soft-coated wheaten terrier
	Italy	bloodhound, Italian greyhound, Maremma sheepdog, Neapolitan mastiff
	Hungary	komondor, kuvasz, puli, vizsla
	Malta	Maltese
	The Netherlands	Keeshond, wirehaired pointing griffon

CONTINENT	COUNTRY	BREED
Europe	Norway	Norwegian elkhound, Lundehund (Norwegian puffin dog), Norwegian buhund
	Portugal	Portuguese water dog
	Russia	borzoi
	Scotland	cairn terrier, golden retriever, Gordon setter, Scottish deerhound, Scottish terrier, Scottish wolfhound, Shetland sheepdog, Skye terrier, West Highland white terrier
	Spain	bichon frise, Ibizan hound, papillon, presa Canario
	Switzerland	Bernese mountain dog, St. Bernard
	Wales	Cardigan Welsh corgi, Pembroke Welsh corgi, Sealyham terrier, Welsh springer spaniel, Welsh terrier
Africa	Egypt	basenji, greyhound, pharaoh hound, saluki
	South Africa	Rhodesian ridgeback
Australia		Australian terrier, Australian cattle dog, silky terrier
Asia and the Middle East	Afghanistan	Afghan hound
	China	Chinese crested, Chinese shar-pei, chow chow, Pekingese, pug
	Japan	Akita, Japanese spaniel, Japanese spitz, shiba inu
	Siberia	Samoyed, Siberian husky
	Tibet	Lhasa apso, shih tzu, Tibetan terrier, Tibetan spaniel, Tibetan mastiff
	Turkey	Anatolian shepherd dog (Kangal dog)

APPENDIX 2

SELECTED BREEDS OF SPORTING DOGS

NAME	ORIGIN	HEIGHT IN INCHES* DOGS (BITCHES)	WEIGHT IN POUNDS* DOGS (BITCHES)	CHARACTERISTICS	COMMENTS
American cocker spaniel	U.S.	15 (14)	24–29 (same)	long coat with thick feathering on legs and belly	originally used in hunting; now primarily a pet or show dog
Brittany	France	17.5–20.5 (same)	30–40 (same)	tailless or short tail; flat, fine coat	similar to a setter; originally named Brittany spaniel
Chesapeake Bay retriever	U.S.	23–26 (21–24)	65–80 (55–70)	dense, coarse coat; strong, powerful body	excellent duck hunter
Clumber spaniel	France	19–20 (17–19)	70–85 (55–70)	white coat; long, heavy body; massive head	popular among British royalty
English cocker spaniel	England	16–17 (15–16)	28–34 (26–32)	solid, compact body; coat is less feathered than its American counterpart	popular since the 19th century; noted for its balance

NAME	ORIGIN	HEIGHT IN INCHES* DOGS (BITCHES)	WEIGHT IN POUNDS* DOGS (BITCHES)	CHARACTERISTICS	COMMENTS
English cocker spaniel	England	16–17 (15–16)	28–34 (26–32)	solid, compact body; coat is less feathered than its American counterpart	popular since the 19th century; noted for its balance
English setter	England	24–25 (same)	40–70 (same)	flecked with color; long head	mellow disposition; valued as gun dog and companion
English springer spaniel	England	20 (19)	50 (40)	medium-sized; docked tail; moderately long coat	noted for endurance and agility
German shorthaired pointer	Germany	23–25 (21–23)	55–70 (45–60)	medium-sized; deep chest; broad ears	long-lived; versatile hunter and all-purpose gun dog

NAME	ORIGIN	HEIGHT IN INCHES* DOGS (BITCHES)	WEIGHT IN POUNDS* DOGS (BITCHES)	CHARACTERISTICS	COMMENTS
Golden retriever	Scotland	23–24 (21.5–22.5)	65–75 (55–65)	powerful body; water-repellent coat in various shades of gold	noted for gentle and affectionate nature
Irish setter	Ireland	27 (25)	70 (60)	elegant build; mahogany or chestnut coat with feathering on ears, legs, belly, and chest	physically most pointerlike of the setters
Labrador retriever	Canada	22.5–24.5 (21.5–23.5)	65–80 (55–70)	medium-sized; muscular build; otter-like tail	popular in England and U.S.; working gun dog, often used as guide or rescue dog
Pointer	England	25–28 (23–26)	55–75 (44–65)	muscular build; tapered tail; short, dense coat	acquire hunting instinct at about two months of age

NAME	ORIGIN	HEIGHT IN INCHES* DOGS (BITCHES)	WEIGHT IN POUNDS* DOGS (BITCHES)	CHARACTERISTICS	COMMENTS
Vizsla	Hungary	22–24 (21–23)	40–60 (same)	medium-sized; light build; short, smooth coat in various shades of golden rust	nearly extinct at end of World War I; short-haired and wirehaired varieties
Weimaraner	Germany	25–27 (23–25)	70–85 (same)	gray coat; medium-sized; graceful	dates to early 19th century

*1 inch = 2.54 centimetres; 1 pound = 0.454 kilogram

APPENDIX 3

SELECTED BREEDS OF HOUNDS					
NAME	ORIGIN	HEIGHT IN INCHES* DOGS (BITCHES)	WEIGHT IN POUNDS* DOGS (BITCHES)	CHARACTERISTICS	COMMENTS
Afghan hound	Afghanistan	27 (25)	60 (50)	regal appearance; curved tail; straight, long coat	celebrated show dog
Basenji	Central Africa	17 (16)	24 (22)	small-sized; wrinkled forehead; tightly curled tail	barkless; admired by Egyptian pharaohs
Basset hound	France	12–14 (same)	40–60 (same)	short-legged; heavy-boned; large head; long, drooping ears	bred by monks in the Middle Ages
Beagle	England	2 varieties, 13 and 15 (same)	18 and 30 (same)	small-sized but solid; short coat	long-lived; excels at rabbit hunting

NAME	ORIGIN	HEIGHT IN INCHES* DOGS (BITCHES)	WEIGHT IN POUNDS* DOGS (BITCHES)	CHARACTERISTICS	COMMENTS
Black and tan coonhound	U.S.	25–27 (23–25)	60–100 (same)	medium to large in size; rangy; long ears	used primarily for tracking and treeing raccoons
Bloodhound	Belgium/ France	25–27 (23–25)	90–110 (80–100)	large-sized; loose skin with folds around head and neck; eyes set deep in orbits	known for its tracking ability; first recorded use by organized law enforcement, England, 1805
Borzoi	Russia	at least 28 (at least 26)	75–105 (60–85)	large-sized; elegant appearance; long, silky coat	popular with Russian nobility; therefore, many were killed after Russian Revolution

NAME	ORIGIN	HEIGHT IN INCHES* DOGS (BITCHES)	WEIGHT IN POUNDS* DOGS (BITCHES)	CHARACTERISTICS	COMMENTS
Dachshund (standard)	Germany	7–10 (same)	16–32 (same)	long-bodied with short legs; three types of coat: smooth, wire-haired, or longhaired	developed around the 1600s; also miniature variety
Greyhound	Egypt	25–27 (same)	65–70 (60–65)	sleek, mus-cled body; short, smooth coat	fastest breed of dog, reach-ing speeds of 45 mph
Irish wolfhound	Ireland	mini-mum 32; aver-age 32–34 (mini-mum 30)	mini-mum 120 (mini mum 105)	large-sized; wiry, rough coat; graceful body	tallest breed of dog

NAME	ORIGIN	HEIGHT IN INCHES* DOGS (BITCHES)	WEIGHT IN POUNDS* DOGS (BITCHES)	CHARACTERISTICS	COMMENTS
Norwegian elkhound	Norway	21 (19)	55 (48)	medium-sized; tightly curled tail; prick ears	hardy; believed to have originated in 5000 BC
Saluki	Egypt	23–28 (may be considerably smaller)	45–60 (proportionately less)	graceful, slender body; long ears	"royal dog of Egypt"; one of the oldest known breeds of domesticated dogs
Whippet	England	19–22 (18–21)	28 (same)	medium-sized; slim but powerful body; long, arched neck	developed to chase rabbits for sport

*1 inch = 2.54 centimetres; 1 pound = 0.454 kilogram

APPENDIX 4

SELECTED BREEDS OF TERRIERS

NAME	ORIGIN	HEIGHT IN INCHES* DOGS (BITCHES)	WEIGHT IN POUNDS* DOGS (BITCHES)	CHARACTERISTICS	COMMENTS
Airedale terrier	England	23 (slightly smaller)	40–50 (same)	black and tan; wiry, dense coat; well-muscled	noted for its intelligence; used in law enforcement
American Stafford-shire terrier	England	18–19 (17–18)	40–50 (same)	stocky, muscular build; short ears; pronounced cheek muscles	originally bred for fighting; excellent guard dog
Bedlington terrier	England	17 (15)	17–23 (same)	curly, lamb-like coat; ears have fur-tasseled tips	originally bred for hunting; noted for its endurance
Border terrier	England	13 (same)	13–15.5 (11.5–14)	otter-like head; hard, wiry, weather-resistant coat	excellent watchdog

NAME	ORIGIN	HEIGHT IN INCHES* DOGS (BITCHES)	WEIGHT IN POUNDS* DOGS (BITCHES)	CHARACTERISTICS	COMMENTS
Bull terrier	England	two sizes: 10–14 and 21–22	24–33 and 50–60	long, egg-shaped head; erect ears; coloured or solid white	(aka pit bull) athletic breed; playful; originally developed as a fighting dog
Cairn terrier	Scotland	10 (9.5)	14 (13)	small-sized but well-muscled; short legs; erect ears; wide, furry face	long-lived
Fox terrier (smooth coat)	England	maximum 15 (slightly smaller)	18 (16)	folded ears; white with black or black-and-tan markings	noted for its remarkable eyesight and keen nose; also wire coat variety

NAME	ORIGIN	HEIGHT IN INCHES* DOGS (BITCHES)	WEIGHT IN POUNDS* DOGS (BITCHES)	CHARACTERISTICS	COMMENTS
Jack Russell terrier	England	two sizes: 10–12 and 12–14	11–13 and 13–17	two varieties: smooth or rough; white with brown, black, or red markings; longer legs than other terriers	developed by Rev. John Russell for foxhunting; courageous and energetic
Kerry blue terrier	Ireland	18–19.5 (17.5–19)	33–40 (proportionately less)	soft, wavy coat; muscular body; born black but matures to gray-blue	long-lived
Miniature schnauzer	Germany	12–14 (same)	13–15 (same)	robust build; rectangular head with thick beard, mustache, and brows	excels in obedience competitions
Scottish terrier	Scotland	10 (same)	19–22 (18–21)	small, compact body; short legs; erect ears; black, wheaten, or brindle	also called Scottie; excellent watchdog and vermin controller

NAME	ORIGIN	HEIGHT IN INCHES* DOGS (BITCHES)	WEIGHT IN POUNDS* DOGS (BITCHES)	CHARACTERISTICS	COMMENTS
Sealyham terrier	Wales	10 (same)	23–35 (same)	white coat, short and sturdy	bred for courage and stamina
Skye terrier	Scotland	10 (9.5)	24 (same)	long, low body; prick or drop ears; long coat veils forehead and eyes	noted for its loyalty
Soft-coated wheaten terrier	Ireland	18–19 (17–18)	35–40 (30–35)	medium-sized; square outline; soft, silky coat	matures late
West Highland white terrier	Scotland	11 (10)	13–19 (same)	small-sized; rough, wiry coat; small, erect ears	originally called Roseneath terrier; bred white after dark-coloured dog was accidentally shot while hunting

*1 inch = 2.54 centimetres; 1 pound = 0.454 kilogram

APPENDIX 5

SELECTED BREEDS OF WORKING DOGS					
NAME	ORIGIN	HEIGHT IN INCHES* DOGS (BITCHES)	WEIGHT IN POUNDS* DOGS (BITCHES)	CHARACTERISTICS	COMMENTS
Akita	Japan	26–28 (24–26)	75–110 or more (same)	large-sized; massive, triangular head; curved tail	originally bred to hunt bears
Alaskan Malamute	U.S.	25 (23)	85 (75)	strong, well-muscled body; thick, coarse coat; broad head with triangular ears	one of the oldest sled dogs
Bernese mountain dog	Switzerland	25–27.5 (23–26)	88 (same)	large-sized; thick, moderately long coat; black with rust and white markings	originally bred to pull carts and drive cows
Boxer	Germany	22.5–25 (21–23.5)	60–70 (same)	medium-sized; square body; blunt muzzle; cropped ears, long and tapered	bred from several breeds, including Great Dane and bulldog

NAME	ORIGIN	HEIGHT IN INCHES* DOGS (BITCHES)	WEIGHT IN POUNDS* DOGS (BITCHES)	CHARACTERISTICS	COMMENTS
Bullmastiff	England	25–27 (24–26)	110–130 (100–120)	well-muscled body; short, dense coat; large, wrinkled head	60% mastiff, 40% bulldog
Doberman pinscher	Germany	26–28 (24–26)	60–88 (same)	medium-sized; sleek, muscular body; typically erect ears	intelligent breed; quick learner
Great Dane	Germany	not less than 30, 32+ preferred (not less than 28, 30+ preferred)	120+ (same)	regal appearance; large, powerful body; massive, expressive head	tallest mastiff breed
Great Pyrenees	Asia	25–32 (same)	90–125 (same)	massive, rugged build; white coat	bred to be a cattle and sheep guardian; loyal and protective

NAME	ORIGIN	HEIGHT IN INCHES* DOGS (BITCHES)	WEIGHT IN POUNDS* DOGS (BITCHES)	CHARACTERISTICS	COMMENTS
Newfoundland	Canada	28 (26)	130–150 (100–120)	large-sized; water-resistant coat; rudderlike tail; webbed feet	noted for its life-saving abilities, particularly in water
Rottweiler	Germany	24–27 (22–25)	90–110 (same)	compact, powerful body; black with rust markings	used as a guard dog and police dog
Saint Bernard	Switzerland	minimum 27.5 (minimum 25)	110–200 (same)	large-sized; red and white coat; powerful head	pathfinder and rescue dog
Samoyed	Siberia	21–24 (19–21)	50–65 (same)	huskylike; double-coated; white, white and biscuit, cream, or all biscuit in colour	people-oriented breed
Siberian husky	northeastern Asia	21–24 (20–22)	45–60 (35–50)	medium-sized; brush tail; small, erect ears	originally called Chukchi

*1 inch = 2.54 centimetres; 1 pound = 0.454 kilogram

APPENDIX 6

SELECTED BREEDS OF HERDING DOGS

NAME	ORIGIN	HEIGHT IN INCHES* DOGS (BITCHES)	WEIGHT IN POUNDS* DOGS (BITCHES)	CHARACTERISTICS	COMMENTS
Australian cattle dog	Australia	18–20 (17–19)	35–45 (same)	sturdy, compact body; moderately short, weather-resistant coat	bred from several breeds, including dingoes and Dalmatians
Australian shepherd	U.S.	20–23 (18–21)	35–70 (same)	medium-sized; lithe and agile; moderate-length coat; bobbed tail	descended from shepherds of Basque region (Spain/France)
Bearded collie	Scotland	21–22 (20–21)	40–60 (same)	medium-sized; muscular body; shaggy, harsh outercoat	dates to the 1500s

NAME	ORIGIN	HEIGHT IN INCHES* DOGS (BITCHES)	WEIGHT IN POUNDS* DOGS (BITCHES)	CHARACTERISTICS	COMMENTS
Belgian sheepdog (Groenendael)	Belgium	24–26 (22–24)	50–60 (same)	well-muscled, square body; erect ears; black coat	used during World War I as message carriers and ambulance dogs; three other varieties
Border collie	England	19–22 (18–21)	31–50 (same)	medium-sized; muscular, athletic build; numerous colours with various combinations of patterns and markings	world's outstanding sheep herder; possesses hypnotic stare used to direct herds
Bouvier des Flandres	Belgium/ France	23.5–27.5 (23.5–26.5)	88 (same)	rugged, compact body; rough coat; blocky head with mustache and beard	natural guard dog, often used in military settings

NAME	ORIGIN	HEIGHT IN INCHES* DOGS (BITCHES)	WEIGHT IN POUNDS* DOGS (BITCHES)	CHARACTERISTICS	COMMENTS
Cardigan Welsh corgi	Wales	10–12 (same)	25–38 (25–34)	long, low body and tail; deep chest; large, prominent ears	not as prevalent as its Pembroke counterpart
Collie (rough)	Scotland	24–26 (22–24)	60–75 (50–65)	lithe body; deep, wide chest; abundant coat, especially on mane and frill	also smooth variety with short coat
German shepherd	Germany	24–26 (22–24)	75–95 (same)	well-muscled, long body; erect ears; long muzzle	one of the most recognized dog breeds
Old English sheepdog	England	minimum 22 (minimum 21)	55+ (same)	compact, square body; profuse, shaggy coat	loud, distinctive bark
Pembroke Welsh corgi	Wales	10–12 (same)	25–38 (same)	low-set body, not as long as Cardigan; docked tail	popular with British royalty; smallest herding dog

NAME	ORIGIN	HEIGHT IN INCHES* DOGS (BITCHES)	WEIGHT IN POUNDS* DOGS (BITCHES)	CHARACTERISTICS	COMMENTS
Puli	Hungary	17 (16)	30 (same)	medium-sized; long, coarse coat that forms cords	named for Puli Hou ("Destroyer Huns")
Shetland sheepdog	Scotland	13–16 (same)	N/A	small-sized; long, rough coat, especially abundant on mane and frill	traces to the border collie; excels in obedience competitions

*1 inch = 2.54 centimetres; 1 pound = 0.454 kilogram

APPENDIX 7

SELECTED BREEDS OF TOY DOGS					
NAME	**ORIGIN**	**HEIGHT IN INCHES* DOGS (BITCHES)**	**WEIGHT IN POUNDS* DOGS (BITCHES)**	**CHARACTERISTICS**	**COMMENTS**
Cavalier King Charles spaniel	England	12–13 (same)	13–18 (same)	moderately long coat with feathering on ears, chest, tail, and legs; large, round eyes	most popular toy dog in England
Chihuahua	Mexico	5 (same)	maximum 6 (same)	large, erect ears; coats are either short and smooth or long and soft with fringing	smallest recognized dog breed
Chinese crested	China	11–13 (same)	5–10 (same)	two coat types: hairless (except for tufts on head, feet, and tail) and powderpuff (long, silky coat)	possesses a harefoot that can grasp and hold objects
Maltese	Malta	5 (same)	4–7 (same)	long, silky, white coat; sturdy build	noted for its fearlessness

NAME	ORIGIN	HEIGHT IN INCHES* DOGS (BITCHES)	WEIGHT IN POUNDS* DOGS (BITCHES)	CHARACTERISTICS	COMMENTS
Papillon	France/ Belgium	8–11 (same)	maximum 11 (same)	fine-boned and dainty; long, silky coat	named for ears that resemble butterfly wings
Pekingese	China	6–9 (same)	maximum 14 (same)	long, coarse coat with heavy feathering; black-masked face with short muzzle	considered sacred in ancient China
Pomeranian	Germany	6–7 (same)	3–7 (same)	cobby body; abundant double coat; small, erect ears	descended from sled dogs of Iceland and Lapland
Pug	China	10–11 (same)	14–18 (same)	square, cobby body; massive head; tightly curled tail; wrinkled face and neck	miniature mastiff

NAME	ORIGIN	HEIGHT IN INCHES* DOGS (BITCHES)	WEIGHT IN POUNDS* DOGS (BITCHES)	CHARACTERISTICS	COMMENTS
Shih tzu	Tibet	10 (same)	9–16 (same)	sturdy build; long, flowing coat; proud carriage	considered a non-sporting dog in Canada
Yorkshire terrier	England	8–9 (same)	maximum 7 (same)	long, silky coat, parted on the face and from the base of the skull to the end of the tail, hanging straight down each side of the body	also called Yorkie; noted for its independent nature

*1 inch = 2.54 centimetres; 1 pound = 0.454 kilogram

APPENDIX 8

SELECTED BREEDS OF NONSPORTING DOGS					
NAME	ORIGIN	HEIGHT IN INCHES* DOGS (BITCHES)	WEIGHT IN POUNDS* DOGS (BITCHES)	CHARACTERISTICS	COMMENTS
Bichon frise	Mediterranean region	9–12 (same)	N/A	small, sturdy body; white, loosely curled coat that resembles powderpuff; plumed tail	depicted in paintings by Francisco de Goya
Boston terrier	U.S.	15–17 (same)	15–25 (same)	compact body; short tail and head; brindle, seal, or black with white markings	one of the few dog breeds that originated in the U.S.
Bulldog	England	13–15 (same)	50 (40)	medium-sized; low-slung body; large head with protruding lower jaw	originally bred to fight bulls

NAME	ORIGIN	HEIGHT IN INCHES* DOGS (BITCHES)	WEIGHT IN POUNDS* DOGS (BITCHES)	CHARACTERISTICS	COMMENTS
Chinese shar-pei	China	18–20 (same)	45–60 (same)	medium-sized; loose skin and wrinkles covering head, neck, and body; broad muzzle	dates to about 200 BC; originally a fighting dog
Chow chow	China	17–20 (same)	45–70 (same)	powerful, square body; large head; blue-black tongue	one of the oldest recog-nized dog breeds; rough-and smooth-coat varieties
Dalmatian	Croatia	19–23 (same)	50–55 (same)	white with black or liver-brown spots; strong, mus-cular build	puppies are born solid white and develop spots as they age

NAME	ORIGIN	HEIGHT IN INCHES* DOGS (BITCHES)	WEIGHT IN POUNDS* DOGS (BITCHES)	CHARACTERISTICS	COMMENTS
Keeshond	The Nether-lands	18 (17)	55–66 (same)	stand-off coat, thick around neck; plumed tail curled on back; small, pointed ears	national dog of Holland; named for 18th-century Dutch patriot
Lhasa apso	Tibet	10–11 (slightly smaller)	13–15 (same)	small-sized; heavy, straight coat that extends over eyes; well-feathered tail carried on back	token of good luck in ancient China
Poodle (standard)	possibly Germany	mini-mum 15 (same)	45–70 (same)	small, square body; dense, curly coat often clipped in a variety of patterns	national dog of France; also toy and miniature varieties
Schipperke	Belgium	11–13 (10–12)	maxi-mum 18 (same)	cobby body; docked tail; black coat; foxlike face	considered one of the best house dogs

*1 inch = 2.54 centimetres; 1 pound = 0.454 kilogram

APPENDIX 9

SELECTED SHORTHAIR BREEDS OF CATS			
NAME	**ORIGIN**	**CHARACTERISTICS**	**COMMENTS**
Abyssinian	probably Egypt	regal appearance; lithe body with long, slender legs	resembles the sacred cat of ancient Egypt
American Shorthair	U.S.	broad, muscular body; thick, dense fur	hardy; natural hunter
American Wirehair	U.S.	medium to large in size; curly coat	rare outside the U.S.
Bengal	U.S.	spotted coat; hind legs shorter than forelegs	cross between Asian leopard cat and American Shorthair tabby
Bombay	U.S.	elegant appearance; resembles Indian black leopard	cross between Burmese and black American Shorthair
British Shorthair	England	broad body with short legs; short, thick tail	oldest natural English breed; many varieties
Burmese	Burma	medium-sized; glossy, thick coat	related to the Siamese
Chartreux	France	robust; all shades of blue-gray	one of the oldest natural breeds
Cornish Rex	England	curly, short coat; large ears	named after the Rex rabbit
Devon Rex	England	coat slightly coarser than Cornish Rex; pixie face	nicknamed "poodle cat"

NAME	ORIGIN	CHARACTERISTICS	COMMENTS
Egyptian Mau	Egypt	graceful body; distinct spot pattern and banded tail	mau is Egyptian for "cat"
Japanese Bobtail	Japan	triangular head with large ears; rabbitlike tail	symbol of good luck
Korat	Thailand	silver-blue coat; heart-shaped face	native name Si-Sawat; considered to be good luck
Manx	Isle of Man	tailless or with stump; double coat	tailless gene can cause skeletal defects and stillbirths if not bred with a tailed cat
Ocicat	U.S.	typically cream coat with dark or light brown spots and markings	cross between Abyssinian and Siamese
Oriental Shorthair	U.S., U.K.	long, lithe body; vivid green eyes	numerous colours unique to the breed
Russian Blue	Russia	blue with silver tipping; plush, double coat; fine-boned, but muscular	considered omens of good luck
Scottish Fold	Scotland	typically folded ears; short, round, well-padded body	folded ear gene can cause crippling when two such types are mated

NAME	ORIGIN	CHARACTERISTICS	COMMENTS
Siamese	Asia	sapphire-blue eyes; long, lean body	noted for its intelligence and unpredictable behaviour
Sphynx	Canada	hairless; large ears	rare outside North America
Tonkinese	U.S.	blue-green eyes; medium-sized	cross between Siamese and Burmese

APPENDIX 10

SELECTED LONGHAIR BREEDS OF CATS			
NAME	**ORIGIN**	**CHARACTERISTICS**	**COMMENTS**
Balinese	U.S.	long, svelte body; sapphire-blue eyes	mutation of Siamese; tail sways when walking, resembling Balinese dancers
Birman	Burma	deep blue eyes; bushy tail; white-gloved paws	known as the "Sacred Cat of Burma"
Cymric	Canada	stout with heavy chest; tailless	a longhair Manx
Himalayan, or Colourpoint Longhair	U.S., Europe	cobby body; short, full tail; sapphire-blue eyes	cross between Siamese and Persian
Javanese	U.S.	graceful with long, lithe body; silky coat	cross between Balinese and Colourpoint Shorthair
Maine Coon cat	U.S.	large and well-muscled; shaggy coat	oldest American breed
Norwegian Forest cat	Norway	robust, muscular body; double coat	featured prominently in Nordic fables of the mid-1800s
Persian	exact origin unknown, possibly Iran	cobby body; massive head	one of the oldest and most popular breeds; many varieties

NAME	ORIGIN	CHARACTERISTICS	COMMENTS
Ragdoll	U.S.	heavy and powerful build; blue eyes	relaxes muscles when picked up, resembling a floppy ragdoll
Somali	U.S.	lithe and muscular body; green or golden eyes; full brush tail	a longhair Abyssinian
Turkish Angora	Turkey	long, plumed tail; large, pointed ears	one of the first longhair cats in Europe

GLOSSARY

aborigine Australian Aborigines are indigenous people of that continent whose ancestors came from Asia at least 50,000 years ago.

altruist Animal displaying behaviour that does not enhance its survival, but the behaviour benefits others of its species.

animal husbandry Controlled cultivation, management, and production of domestic animals, including improvement of the qualities considered desirable by humans by means of breeding. Animals are bred and raised for utility (e.g., food, fur), sport, pleasure, and research.

animism Doctrine that the vital principle of organic development is immaterial spirit.

baculum A slender bone reinforcing the penis in many mammals.

blastomycosis Disease of people and less often of other animals caused by yeast fungus (*Blastomyces dermititidis*) that primarily affects the lungs and skin.

bubonic plague Acute and severe infection caused by the rod-shaped bacterium *Yersinia pestis* (sometimes categorized as *Pasteurella pestis*) that occurs mainly in wild rodents, such as rats or squirrels.

cache Hiding place.

carnassial Of, relating to, or being teeth of a carnivorous mammal that are larger and longer than adjacent teeth and adapted for cutting rather than tearing.

chaparral Dense impenetrable thicket of shrubs or dwarf trees.

cohort Group of individuals of the same age or possessing some other factor in common.

dam Female parent—used especially regarding a domestic animal.

deciduous Falling off or shedding at the end of the growing period.

decimate To destroy a considerable part of: to reduce to the point of almost complete extermination.

dentition The character of the teeth as determined by their form and arrangement.

depredate Prey upon.

dewclaw Vestigial digit not reaching to the ground on the foot of a mammal.

dhole Fierce wild dog (*Cuon dukhunensis*) of Asia that hunts in packs and may attack even large and ferocious animals (as the tiger).

distemper A highly contagious virus disease of canines and especially of dogs that is caused by a morbillivirus (species Canine distemper virus) and is marked by a low white blood cell count, fever, and respiratory gastrointestinal, and neurological symptoms—called also canine distemper.

diurnal Active chiefly in the daytime.

effluvium An invisible emanation; especially : an offensive exhalation or smell.

endocrine Of, relating to, or associated with a hormone.

erectile Capable of being raised to an upright position.

estrus A regularly recurrent state of sexual excitability during which the female of most mammals will accept the male and is capable of conceiving.

ethologist One who engages in the scientific and objective study of animal behaviour especially under natural conditions.

extirpate To destroy completely; wipe out.

fauna All the species of animals found in a particular region, period, or special environment.

feline infectious peritonitis (FIP) Almost invariably fatal infectious disease of cats characterized by fever, weight loss, and appetite loss.

feral Not domesticated or cultivated: wild.

fledged Feathered and capable of flight.

frugivorous Feeding on fruit.

grizzled Sprinkled or streaked with gray.

guanine Organic compound belonging to the purine group, a class of compounds with a characteristic two-ringed structure, composed of carbon and nitrogen atoms, and occurring free or combined in such diverse natural sources as guano (the accumulated excrement and dead bodies of birds, bats, and seals), sugar beets, yeast, and fish scales.

harefoot Long narrow close-toed foot characteristic of some dogs, including the American foxhound and the Chinese crested.

heartworm Serious yet preventable mosquito-borne disease of dogs and cats caused by a parasitic worm, the adults of which colonize the right ventricle of the heart and the pulmonary artery.

infanticide The killing of an infant.

insectivorous Depending on insects as food.

leptospirosis Also called pea picker's disease or swineherd's disease, acute systemic illness of animals, occasionally communicable to humans, that is characterized by extensive inflammation of the blood vessels.

Lyme disease Tick-borne bacterial disease that was first conclusively identified in 1975 and is named for the town in Connecticut, U.S., in which it was first observed.

mange Skin disease of animals caused by mite infestations, characterized by inflammation, itching, thickening of the skin, and hair loss.

mangrove Any tropical tree or shrub of the genus Rhizophora growing in marshes or tidal shores, noted for their interlacing above-ground roots.

masseter Large muscle that raises the lower jaw and assists in mastication (chewing).

mast Nuts (as acorns) accumulated on the forest floor and often serving as food for animals.

nonretractile Not capable of being drawn back in; nonretractable.

omnivorous Feeding on both animal and vegetable substances.

opacity Opaque spot in a normally transparent structure (as the lens of the eye).

parvovirus A highly contagious virus disease of dogs that is spread especially by contact with infected feces. Canine parvovirus causes acute illness in dogs in the form of fever, bloody diarrhea, vomiting, and dehydration.

peccary Any of several largely nocturnal gregarious American mammals resembling the related pigs.

pelage Hairy, woolly, or furry coat of a mammal, distinguished from the underlying bare skin.

perineum Area of tissue between the anus and the posterior part of the external genitalia. A perineal gland is one in this region.

polygyny The condition of having more than one female mate at one time.

predation A mode of life in which food is primarily obtained by the killing and consuming of animals.

protrusible Capable of jutting out from the surrounding surface.

rabies Acute, ordinarily fatal, viral disease of the central nervous system that is usually spread among domestic dogs and wild carnivorous animals by a bite. All warm-blooded animals, including humans, are susceptible to rabies infection.

silage Stored fermented fodder, as that found in a silo.

snowpack Seasonal accumulation of slow-melting packed snow.

taiga Open coniferous forest growing on swampy ground that is commonly covered with lichens.

talisman Object held to act as a charm to avert evil and bring good fortune.

taxonomy Classification; especially: orderly classification of plants and animals according to their presumed natural relationships. Taxon (plural taxa) is the name applied to any taxonomic group.

terrestrial Of or relating to the earth or its inhabitants.

toxoplasmosis Infection of tissue cells of the central nervous system, spleen, liver, and other organs by a parasite, *Toxoplasma gondii*. Infection occurs in domestic and wild animals, birds, and humans and is worldwide in distribution.

trophic Of or relating to nutrition or a specific feeding level within an ecosystem.

ungulate Hoofed typically herbivorous quadruped mammal (as a pig, camel, hippopotamus, horse, rhinoceros, or elephant) of a polyphyletic group formerly considered a major mammalian taxon (Ungulata).

vector A disease-transmitting organism (as an insect).

vulva External parts of the female genital organs.

zygote Fertilized egg cell that results from the union of a female gamete (egg, or ovum) with a male gamete (sperm).

BIBLIOGRAPHY

CARNIVORES

For general information on the biology of the carnivores, see Ronald M. Nowak (ed.), *Walker's Carnivores of the World* (2005), adapted from Ronald M. Nowak (ed.), *Walker's Mammals of the World*, 6th ed., (1999), in which each family and genus of order Carnivora is described and illustrated in turn. R.F. Ewer, *The Carnivores* (1973, reissued 1985), describes each family of Carnivora within the context of anatomy, physiology, and behaviour. John L. Gittleman (ed.), *Carnivore Behavior, Ecology, and Evolution*, 2 vol. (1989–96); and John L. Gittleman, Stephan M. Funk, David W. MacDonald, and Robert K. Wayne (eds.), *Carnivore Conservation* (2001), gather essays offering the most modern understanding of Carnivora.

DOGS

The American Kennel Club, *The Complete Dog Book*, 20th ed. (2006), comprehensively illustrates every breed that is registerable in the AKC stud book and includes a chapter on health care and puppy management. David Taylor and Connie Vanacore, *The Ultimate Dog Book* (1990), is an illustrated overview of most of the breeds registered in the United States and Great Britain, with brief histories and descriptions of each.

Stanley J. Olsen, *Origins of the Domestic Dog* (1985), is an anthropological study of fossils, primarily in the United States. Maxwell Riddle, *The Wild Dogs in Life and Legend* (1979), describes many wild canids that exist in different parts of the world and relates the stories natives tell about them.

A vastly important contribution to the understanding of canine behaviour is John Paul Scott and John L. Fuller, *Genetics and the Social Behavior of the Dog* (1965, reissued as *Dog Behavior: The Genetic Basis*, 1974), describing the genetic structure of personality based on original research by the authors. The foundational work describing the development of personality in puppies is Clarence J. Pfaffenberger, *The New Knowledge of Dog Behavior* (1963), based on research done by Scott and Fuller in the 1950s. Jack Volhard and Melissa Bartlett, *What All Good Dogs Should Know* (1991), is a basic primer for obedience training. Carol Lea Benjamin, *Mother Knows Best: The Natural Way to Train Your Dog* (1985), uses a common-sense approach to teaching basic manners and solving problems.

William J. Kay and Elizabeth Randolph, *The Complete Book of Dog Health* (1985), gives detailed descriptions of the major organ systems of the dog and describes common ailments and symptoms that dog owners can identify. Harold R. Spira, *Canine Terminology* (1982), definitively describes canine anatomy, illustrated from nose to tail. Terri McGinnis, *The Well Dog Book* (1991), is a basic veterinary manual for dog owners. Also helpful is Malcolm B. Willis, *Practical Genetics for Dog Breeders* (1992), which studies the genetic structure of the dog, including anatomy, coat colour, and breed differentiation.

WOLVES

L. David Mech, *The Wolf: The Ecology and Behavior of an Endangered Species* (1970, reissued 1981), remains a scientific yet readable account of the author's research on wolves. Rick McIntyre, *A Society of Wolves: National Parks and the Battle over the Wolf*, rev. ed. (1996), examines the debate over the 1995 reintroduction of wolves into Yellowstone National Park and the possibility of reintroduction elsewhere. Diana Landau (ed.), *Wolf: Spirit of the Wild* (1993, reissued 2000), compiles a variety of writings and graphics to portray wolves in the context of human cultures. Ludwig N. Carbyn, Steven H. Fritts, and Dale R. Seip (eds.), *Ecology and Conservation of Wolves in a Changing World* (1995), presents the proceedings of the Second North American Symposium on Wolves.

DOMESTIC CATS

Patricia Dale-Green, *Cult of the Cat* (1963, reissued as *The Archetypal Cat,* 1983), is a historical study of humankind's long relationship with felines. Cat behaviour is discussed in Michael W. Fox, *Understanding Your Cat* (1974), a book for the layperson; Dennis C. Turner and Patrick Bateson (eds.), *The Domestic Cat: The Biology of Its Behavior* (1988), a collection of research studies on various aspects of cat behaviour, for readers with some scientific knowledge; Bonnie Beaver, *Veterinary Aspects of Feline Behavior* (1980), a detailed review of behaviour problems and their interpretation and treatment; and Desmond Morris, *Catwatching* (1986; also published as *Cat Watching,* 1987), an informative and entertaining book.

Books on cats as pets include Muriel Beadle, *The Cat* (1977); Gino Pugnetti, *Simon and Schuster's Guide to Cats, trans. from Italian,* ed. by Mordecai Siegal (1983), a useful handbook for cat owners; William J. Kay and Elizabeth Randolph, *The Complete Book of Cat Health* (1985); Terri McGinnis, *The Well Cat Book* (1975), a layperson's guide to cat care; and David Taylor, *You & Your Cat* (1986), which provides excellent advice on cat health maintenance and on recognition of health problems. More technical health-care books include Lon D. Lewis, Mark L. Morris, and Michael S. Hand, *Small Animal Clinical Nutrition*, 3rd ed. (1987), a review of cat and dog nutritional requirements and diet-related health problems; and Robert C. McClure, Mark J. Dallman, and Phillip D. Garrett, *Cat Anatomy* (1973), one of the standard veterinary textbooks. Detailed descriptions of various cat breeds and information about cat clubs and shows in various countries may be found in Grace Pond (ed.), *The Complete Cat Encyclopedia* (1972).

BIG CATS

T.M. Caro, *Cheetahs of the Serengeti Plains: Group Living in an Asocial Species* (1994), summarizes ecological findings of more than a decade of field research and compares solitary and group behaviour of cheetahs with that of other cats.

George B. Schaller, *The Serengeti Lion: A Study of Predator-Prey Relations* (1972, reissued 1976), remains the standard scientific reference for African lions. Craig Packer, *Into Africa* (1994, reissued 1996), provides a more personal view of lion research and updates much of the work begun by Schaller. Pieter Kat and Chris Harvey, *Prides: The Lions of Moremi* (2000), offers stunning photographs and solid scientific content that challenges some ideas put forth by Packer and Schaller.

K. Ullas Karanth, *The Way of the Tiger: Natural History and Conservation of the Endangered Big Cat* (2001), introduces readers to a wide range of scientific and cultural issues relating to the species. John Seidensticker, Sarah Christie, and Peter Jackson (eds.), *Riding the Tiger: Tiger Conservation in Human-Dominated Landscapes* (1999), compiles the work of numerous contributors on the topics of ecology and poaching as they relate to all subspecies.

Peter Mattheissen, *Tigers in the Snow* (2000), describes
the conservation efforts of Russians and Americans col-
laborating on the Siberian Tiger Project.

PANDAS

George B. Schaller et al., *The Giant Pandas of Wolong*
(1985), written with the help of Chinese researchers, is
the first account of panda biology and continues to be
the single most comprehensive source of information on
the species.

INDEX